George Muller

MAN OF FAITH & MIRACLES

A biography of one of the greatest prayer-warriors of the past century

by Basil Miller

DIMENSION BOOKS
Bethany Fellowship, Inc.
Minneapolis, Minnesota

DIMENSION BOOKS
are published by
Bethany Fellowship, Inc.
6820 Auto Club Road
Minneapolis, Minnesota 55438

Copyright, MCMXLI, by
Zondervan Publishing House

Printed in the
United States of America

ISBN 0-87123-182-4

CONTENTS

I. SIN-DARKENED YOUTH 5

II. THE YOUTH LEARNS TO PRAY 14

III. MASTERING LESSONS OF TRUST 23

IV. THE BIRTH OF A NEW IDEA 33

V. INTO HIS LIFE'S WORK AT LAST 43

VI. TRUSTING GOD FOR DAILY SUPPLIES 52

VII. BUILDING FOR GOD AND ORPHANS 65

VIII. UNDERTAKING GREATER THINGS FOR GOD . . . 77

IX. CARRYING FAITH'S MESSAGE TO THE WORLD . . 91

X. THE SCRIPTURAL KNOWLEDGE INSTITUTION . . . 104

XI. TRIALS OF FAITH 114

XII. GIFTS AND GIVING 124

XIII. THE EVENING OF HIS LIFE 137

XIV. HIS LENGTHENING SHADOW 149

CHAPTER I

SIN-DARKENED YOUTH

GEORGE MULLER is literally the "man God made." In his youth there was no religious background. He lived without thought of God or righteousness until suddenly awakened to his need of God's transforming fellowship. He tasted sin's bitter dregs in youth, only to know in manhood that God was "able to do exceedingly, abundantly above all" he thought or asked.

The miracle of his life comes not from a heritage rich in religious values. The key is to be found in the fact that George in his youth opened all avenues of his being to the divine infilling. Henceforth he was a man who lived with eternity in view.

He looked, after the shadow of God's glory rested upon him, beyond time and saw God. Henceforth he was never again to ask man for body or soul needs. He realized that God alone was able, and in that realization the puny supplies of man dwarfed beside the reservoirs of God's grace which he tapped by faith.

He learned the secret of getting things from God, the simple expedient of boldly coming to the throne to receive. He practiced this daily for seventy-three years, and in coming he never found the throne vacant nor the supplies exhausted. He learned not to bind God by the limits of his own faith. He asked, knowing that God, Who heard, was able.

He has been called *the apostle of faith.* The narrative of God's dealings with him has been termed *the life of trust.* But I think of him as *the man God made.* He portrays to the highest degree God in life making. Viewed in light of his sinful youth this becomes God in remaking life.

Let us trace the hand of God through this long career of ninety-three years, eight months and five days, seventy-three years and almost two months of which were walked hand in hand with God.

George was a native of Prussia, born at Kroppenstaedt, on September 27, 1805. Little is known of his first five years, but in 1810 the family moved four miles away where his father became collector of the excise, a form of tax placed upon business houses and individuals for certain privileges. For the next eleven years the Mullers lived at Heimersleben.

"My father," writes George Muller, "who educated his children on worldly principles, gave us much money, considering our age. The result was that it led my brother and me into many sins. Before I was ten years old I repeatedly took of the government money which was intrusted to my father . . . till one day . . . he detected my theft, by depositing a counted sum in the room where I was, and leaving me to myself for awhile. I took some of the money and hid it under my foot in my shoe."

But his father was not to be outdone, for he soon detected the loss, and on searching George found the money. But punishment did not change George's tactics, for repeatedly he stole the government money.

"Though I was punished on this and other occasions, yet I did not remember that anytime . . . it made any other impression upon me than to make me think how I might do the thing the next time more cleverly."

When George was between ten and eleven he was sent to Halberstadt to prepare for the university. His father desired that he should train for the Lutheran ministry. "Not that thus I might serve God, but that I might have a comfortable living," says Mr. Muller writing many years later. Instead of studying as he should, he spent his time reading low class novels and indulging in sinful practices.

When fourteen years of age a tragedy marked his life in the form of his mother's death. The night she was dying, George, being unaware of her illness, was playing cards, and the next day, which was Sunday, went to a tavern with some of his sinful companions. On the following day he received his first religious instruction previous to being confirmed. Thus you see his was an early life devoid of any religious training. Even this first religious instruction was received in a careless manner. He was a light-hearted sinful youth who drank of worldly pleasures to satiation.

His mother's death made no lasting impression upon him. Three or four days before his confirmation, which admitted him to partake of the Lord's Supper, he committed a gross immorality. So deceitful had he become that he could not play square with the minister who confirmed him. "I handed over to him only the twelfth part of the fee which my father had given me for him," he remarks, delineating the downward course of his sins.

"In this state of heart, without prayer, without repentance, without faith, without knowledge of the plan of salvation, I was confirmed, and took the Lord's Supper, on the Sunday after Easter, 1820. . . . Yet

I was not without some feeling. . . . I made resolutions to turn from those vices in which I was living and to study more. But as I had no regard for God, and attempted the thing in my own strength, all soon came to nothing, and I still grew worse."

The following year when his father was transferred to Schoenebeck, George asked to attend the cathedral school at Magdeburg, which was close by. Before attending school in November, he stayed at the home place, superintending some alterations in it and reading the classics with a clergyman named Dr. Nagel. While left thus alone, he collected the money owed his father and spent it upon his sinful pleasures.

In November of 1821, he took a trip to Magdeburg, where for six days he spent his time in "much sin." Taking all the money he could obtain by various ruses he traveled to Brunswick, and lived for a week at an expensive hotel. Money gone, he tried the same trick at a near-by village hotel, where the owner suspecting that he had no money asked him to leave his best clothes as security.

This time he walked about six miles to Wolfenbuttel and at an inn began to live as though he had much money. But this proved to be the sixteen-year-old boy's undoing, for when he sought to escape from a high window he was caught. Confessing the truth, he expected mercy, but there was none.

Immediately he was arrested and taken to a police officer, and later to jail as a vagabond or thief. "I now found myself, at the age of sixteen, an inmate of the same dwelling with thieves and murderers, and treated accordingly. . . . On the second day I asked the keeper for a Bible, not to consider its blessed contents, but to pass away the time," George relates. For twenty-four days—from December 18 to January 12—he was confined to the prison. His father obtained his release by paying the inn debt and his maintenance at the jail, also furnishing enough money for the lad to return home.

In October, 1822, he entered a school at Nordhausen, where he remained for two and a half years studying with diligence the Latin classics, French history, German literature, as well as a little Hebrew, Greek and mathematics. "I used to rise regularly at four, winter and summer, and generally studied all the day, with little exception, till ten at night." His serious life caused him to be held up as an example to the class.

"I did not," he writes, "care in the least about God, but lived secretly in much sin, in consequence of which I was taken ill, and for thirteen weeks confined to my room. During my illness I had no real sorrow of heart. . . . I cared nothing about the Word of God. I had about three hundred books of my own, but no Bible."

His was a student life which found pleasure in the classics, but one devoid of love for the higher things of religion. "I practically," he affirms plumbing the depths of his youthful irreligion, "set a far higher value upon the writings of Horace and Cicero, Voltaire and Moliere, than upon the volume of inspiration."

Now and then tinges of conscience would prick his soul and he would determine to be better, "particularly when I went to the Lord's Supper. . . . The day previous to attending that ordinance I used to refrain from certain things; and on the day itself I was serious. . . . But after one or two days were over, all was forgotten, and I was as bad as ever."

George was a dissipated youth who spent the money

his father furnished, as the other prodigals did, in riotous living. Once when his funds were exhausted, he pretended his money had been stolen, and forcing the lock on his trunk and guitar case, he went to the director's room half dressed, telling the story of the supposed theft. This trick aroused sympathy for him, for as an actor his tale seemed to ring true.

When twenty he became a member of the University of Halle with excellent testimonials, and was granted the privilege of preaching in the Lutheran Establishment. Here he began to realize that unless he reformed, no church would have him as its clergyman and his rating in this profession would be handicapped. He looked upon the clergy as a means of gaining a livelihood, and not as a service.

"I thought," he says, "no parish would choose me as their pastor . . . and without a considerable knowledge of divinity I should never get a good living. But the moment I entered Halle . . . all my resolutions came to nothing . . . I renewed my profligate life afresh, though now a student of divinity . . . I had no sorrow of heart on account of offending God."

One day in his evil career he met a fellow-student by the name of Beta, who formerly had tried to live a Christian life, but whose efforts caused Muller to despise him. "It now appeared well to me to choose him as my friend, thinking that, if I could but have better companions, I should by that means improve my own conduct."

George guessed wrong this time—for *Beta was a backslider!* And Beta sought out George's friendship believing that he would thus be introduced to the pleasures which his wilder companion seemed to enjoy.

God was at work, for it was through Beta that George's redemption was to take place. It was *a* friendship that the studious, though profligate, youth needed, but it was *the* transforming friendship of God, and not of a young man who walked far behind his religious privileges.

"My foolish heart was again deceived," declares Mr. Muller. "And yet God in His abundant mercy made him . . . the instrument of doing me good, not merely for time, but for eternity."

Debauchery demanded its pay and George took seriously ill. His "conduct was outwardly rather better." But this betterment, he avows, came about not because of religious but financial reasons. His money was too limited to meet the toll demanded by an evil life. In August of 1825, he and Beta, along with two other students, borrowed enough money on their belongings to travel through Prussia for a few days, which resulted in a desire to see nature's grander moods in Switzerland.

The lads were confronted by a lack of money and no passports. But the ingenious George soon eliminated these obstacles by borrowing on their books and other possessions, and through false and forged letters from their parents he obtained the passports.

Wickedness was so inground in George's system that even on this trip he was a common thief. "I was on this journey like Judas," George confesses, "for having the common purse, I was a thief. I managed so that the journey cost me but two-thirds of what it cost my friends . . ."

On returning to Prussia the youth visited home, where his old determination to alter his mode of living sprang up again. But when vacation days were over, and new students came to the university, and with money in his pockets once more, he drifted back into his foreboding ways.

But those sin-darkened days were near an end. God in His inscrutable manner had planned a meeting where the divine hand should begin remaking the life that sin had marred. The same friend Beta with whom he had sinned was to be God's instrument in bringing George into the glorious light of the Gospel. Sin's night was almost over and the daydawn of grace was about to burst with transforming beauty over the youth's soul.

"The divine Hand in this history is doubly plain," writes A. T. Pierson in his biography of George Muller, "when we see that this was also the period of preparation for his life-work. . . . During the next ten years we shall watch the divine Potter, to Whom George Muller was a chosen vessel for service, moulding and fitting the vessel for His use. Every step is one of preparation . . ."

"The time was now come when God would have mercy upon me," says Mr. Muller reviewing his soul-blighting course of iniquity. "At a time when I was as careless about Him as ever, He sent His Spirit into my heart. I had no Bible and had not read one for years. I went to church but seldom; but, from custom, I took the Lord's Supper twice a year. I had never heard the gospel preached. I had never met with a person who told me that he meant, by the help of God, to live according to the Holy Scriptures. In short, I had not the least idea that there were any persons really different from myself."

Mr. Muller had come to the parting of the ways. No more was the prodigal to wander after life's dried and sinful husks, but was to walk the backward trail to Father's home, where as a son most blessed he was henceforth to live for God's glory.

This is our last look at the sinful youth, for sin and he no longer had a common set of values.

CHAPTER II

THE YOUTH LEARNS TO PRAY

"I HAD never either seen anyone on his knees, nor had I ever myself prayed on my knees," confesses Mr. Muller. Up till this time his life had been one with little prayer in it. He had not learned the glory that comes from asking God for life's blessings. When he saw a man on his knees, the entire course of his career was changed. He found at last the things for which sinful youth, when driven by religious impulses, had quested.

One Saturday afternoon about the middle of November, 1825, when George was twenty, he and Beta took a walk in the open fields. On returning Beta asked George to attend a cottage meeting with him, which he had been in the habit of attending each Saturday evening at the home of a Christian.

"And what do they do at this meeting?" asked George.

"They read the Bible, sing a few hymns, pray and someone reads a printed sermon."

"No sooner had I heard this than it was to me as if I had found something after which I had been seeking all my life long," says our hero. "We went together in the evening. As I did not know the manners of believers, and the joy they had in seeing poor

14

sinners . . . caring about the things of God, I made an apology for coming."

"Come as often as you please; house and heart are open to you," returned Mr. Wagner, a Christian trades-man, in whose house the meeting was held.

The group sat down and sang a hymn, which was followed by a prayer offered by one of the brothers present, named Kayser—later becoming a missionary to Africa under the London Missionary Society—who called upon God for His blessings to fall on the meet-ing.

That kneeling in prayer made a lasting impression upon Muller.

Off their knees, Kayser read to the company a chapter from the Bible, and then a printed sermon, since it was not lawful for a layman to expound the Scriptures in Prussia. When the benedictory hymn had been sung, the believers again went to their knees, to be led this time in prayer by Wagner.

"I could not pray as well," thought George, as he listened to the tradesman's eloquent pleas, "though I am much more learned than this illiterate man."

He was truly happy for the first time in his life. "If I had been asked why I was happy, I could not have clearly explained it," Muller notes long after he had learned the joy of praying.

Homeward bound George said to his friend Beta, "All we have seen on our journey to Switzerland, and all our former pleasures, are as nothing in comparison with this evening."

At home again the young man fell upon his knees. When it came time to sleep, George says, "I lay peace-ful and happy in my bed."

He had little doubt that God began a work of grace

in his heart, a deep sense of joy springing up with scarcely any sorrow or with but little knowledge. The work of divine grace had been done and henceforth the young man is to walk the path of the just which shines with ever-increasing brightness until it ends in the perfect day.

His was a changed life. He read the Scriptures and not the classics as formerly, praying often, and attended church as prompted by divine love within. At the university he stood on the side of Christ, and gladly paid the price of being laughed at by his fellow-students for his religious fervor.

In January of 1826 he was moved by spiritual ardor to become a missionary, through reading missionary papers, and by meeting Hermann Ball, a learned and wealthy young man, who worked in Poland among the Jews as a missionary.

"I truly began to enjoy," says Mr. Muller, "the peace of God which passeth all understanding." And off went a letter to Father and Mother Muller entreating them to seek the Lord, for they too could be as happy as he. But an angry letter was their answer, for his father desired that he should stop all his nonsense and get to work making out of himself an accepted minister . . . a clergyman with a good living, who would be able to support his parents in their old age.

At the same time the famous Dr. Tholuck took the chair of divinity at the University, and this godly man drew pious students to him. From the professor George received a strengthening influence. At once he determined to be free from his parents, to receive no more money from them, and to trust solely in the Lord for his needs.

God was not long in supplying the temporal needs of this trusting student, for Tholuck shortly recommended him to a group of American professors who did not understand German, to teach them the language. "Thus did the Lord richly make up to me the little which I had relinquished for His sake," says Mr. Muller.

Though a divinity student, he had not yet preached. His first sermon was a severe trial, for he attempted to carry it through on his own strength. A schoolmaster arranged for him to speak in the parish of an aged clergyman, and on August 27, 1826, he went out and spoke at the morning service, having written and memorized his message. The delivery brought no unusual blessing from the Lord. In the afternoon there was another service at which he could speak more freely than in the morning.

"It came to my mind to read the fifth chapter of Matthew, and to make such remarks as I was able. . . . Immediately upon beginning to expound 'Blessed are the poor in spirit,' I felt myself greatly assisted; and whereas in the morning my sermon had not been simple enough for the people to understand it, I now was listened to with the greatest attention. . . . My own peace and joy were great." This endeavor launched him on a preaching career, which henceforth was to be a simple exposition of the Scriptures. From this course he never deviated throughout his many years as a public servant of the Master.

As a divinity student he fell into the common error of reading books about the Bible but not reading the Bible itself. "I practically preferred for the first four years of my divine life the works of uninspired men," he confesses. "The consequence was that I remained a babe, both in knowledge and grace."

Since the ministers were themselves unenlightened spiritually there was little in the sermons to feed his soul. Though he regularly went to church, when not preaching, yet he scarcely ever heard the truth, he affirms, "for there was no enlightened clergyman in the town." He often walked ten or fifteen miles to hear a godly minister expound the Word.

The one bright spot in the week was the meeting in Johann Wagner's home, where he had been spiritually awakened. George also attended a Sunday meeting of religious students, which increased from six to twenty during the time he was at Halle.

He soon took another significant step, which brought him into contact with an orphanage work, later to be the model of his own orphanages. For two months he lived in the free lodgings furnished for divinity students in the famous Orphan Houses built by A. H. Franke. More than a hundred years earlier Franke had been led to establish an orphanage in entire dependence upon God. Though Franke had died in 1727, the work continued through faith. This became an inspiration to Muller and often he records how much he was indebted to the example of trust and prayer which Franke exhibited.

In August of the same year (1827) when George was twenty-two, he heard that the Continental Society in England planned to send a missionary to Bucharest, to assist an aged missionary in his work. After much prayer Mr. Muller offered himself to Dr. Tholuck, who had been requested to find a suited minister for this service.

"Most unexpectedly," writes this fervent soul, "my father gave his consent. . . . I prayed with a degree of earnestness concerning my future work." But God intervened, for this was not the divine will for Muller. The war between the Turks and the Russians caused the society to abandon the idea.

With the outreaching of his soul, the young minister was seeking the field for his life's investment. While there was a ringing challenge to be a missionary, he was never permitted to serve in this capacity, since God had other plans for his life. He had become interested in the Hebrew language to which he was devoting much study.

On November 17, he called upon Dr. Tholuck, who learning of this interest in the youth's life, asked, "Would you like to serve as a missionary to the Jews?" The professor went on to say that he was connected with the London Missionary Society for Promoting Christianity among the Jews.

"I was struck with the question," declares Mr. Muller, "and told him what had passed in my mind."

A divine miracle with far-reaching results was about to occur in Muller's experience from which directly sprang his life's work. Ofttimes God indirectly leads one to the fields of his service, which was to be the case with George. God wanted this youth in England where his sphere of influence was to be centered.

When Tholuck learned that his young student was interested in the Jews, he at once wrote to the London Society suggesting Muller's name as a candidate. In March, 1828, the Society answered asking the candidate a number of questions, and on June 13 a letter came saying that they would take George as a missionary student for six months on probation.

There was one proviso, meaningful and life determining. *He must come to London . . .* for God wanted

George Muller's fame to spread throughout the world from this English-speaking nation. Germany had her Franke and England must also have her Muller, apostle of faith.

There was a formidable obstacle. Every Prussian man must serve three years in the army; and classical students who had passed the university examinations were forced to serve only one year. Muller had not yet received his army training, and without an exemption he could not obtain a passport to leave the country. His application for exemption was denied, and Muller felt much depressed because of the denial. But God had plans for this exemption.

While in Leipsic with an American professor for whom he was serving as tutor in German, between acts at the opera George took some iced refreshments which caused him to become sick. This resulted in a broken blood vessel in his stomach. Being advised by friends to go to Berlin, he found an open door for preaching to wards in the poorhouse and in the prisons.

On February 3, 1829, he was re-examined for the army, and because of his stomach trouble was declared physically unfit for service, and hence exempted. Immediately he received his passport and set sail for London where he arrived on March 19.

While waiting for his missionary appointment in London, he heard friends speak of a dentist, a Mr. Groves, who gave up a salary of $7,500 a year to be a missionary to Persia, simply trusting in God for temporal supplies. "This made an impression on me," Muller affirms, "that I not only marked it down in my journal, but also wrote about it to my German friends."

Again God was gently leading Muller into a life

of trust. His old trouble struck again and for weeks he despaired of his life. "I longed exceedingly to depart and be with Christ," he says.

"O Lord," he prayed while on his sick bed, "do with me as seemeth best"—a prayer which was slowly answered. For God permitted his servant to linger in sickness that his soul might learn a new lesson in trust.

A few days later he went to Tiegnmouth to recuperate. Here the Ebenezer chapel was reopened and Mr. Muller had the privilege of living for ten days with the preacher. It was during this brief stay that God taught him the true meaning of the Bible. "God began to show me," he writes, "that His Word alone is our standard of judgment; that it can be explained only by the Holy Spirit; and that in our day, as well as in former times, He is the teacher of the people."

These few days seemed unmeaningful in building Muller's life career until this lesson appears. For the Bible became, from then on, the true source of his inspiration, and the one book to which he was solely devoted, which proved to be a pivot in the upward climb of George's soul.

He delineates how he tested the Bible truth by experience. "The Lord enabled me to put it to the test of experience, by laying aside commentaries, and almost every other book, and simply reading the Word of God and studying it. The result of this was that the first evening I shut myself into my room to give myself to prayer and meditation over the Scriptures, I learned more in a few hours than I had done during a period of several months previously." He goes on to add, *"But the particular difference was that I received real strength for my soul in doing so."*

This brief stay in the country worked the design of God into his spiritual pilgrimage, for henceforth through meditation upon the Bible and prayer he was to commit his ways unto the Lord. Near the end of his life he affirmed that he had read the Bible through approximately two hundred times, one hundred of which were *on his knees.* This is the keynote of that marvelous life of trust. He found God's promises in the Bible and experienced the truth of them in his everyday life. He learned to believe what he read and to act accordingly. He mined religious truth, not from books of human fabrication, but from God through divine inspiration, and what he read he lived.

God is now ready to thrust Muller forth into his vineyard a full-fledged apostle of trust. Yet there is another lesson he is to experience before God can use him to the fullest extent. He must learn *to tell not man but God his needs* and to believe God will supply them. Around the bend in his career this lesson is next in God's book of life for Muller to master.

Chapter III

MASTERING LESSONS OF TRUST

THE REST at Devonshire acted as a tonic to Muller's worn body, but the greatest blessing came to his soul. His prayer had been that God would bless the journey to the benefit of body and soul. "In the beginning of September (1829) I returned to London, much better in body, and as to my soul, the change was so great that it was like a second conversion."

At once he must find something to do for the Master. He decided to start a prayer meeting for the seminary students, by calling them together for devotions from six until eight each morning. His soul became so enrapt with the joy of prayer after these services that throughout the day he lingered long before God's throne. Often in the evening at family devotions he would continue until midnight praying, in the morning to awake and call the students to the six o'clock meeting again.

Becoming impatient at his missionary inactivity, he asked the Society to allot him work to do among the Jews, but when the letter brought no response he started his labors, whether officially appointed or not. He distributed tracts, taught a Sunday school class of Jewish boys with about fifty in attendance, and read the Bible to them.

While waiting to be sent out into God's work by

man, Mr. Muller was led by the Spirit to feel that this waiting for appointment was wrong; that instead he should receive orders only from the Holy Spirit as Paul and Barnabas were sent forth. He wrote the Society while spending the Christmas vacation with some friends at Devon, and frankly stated his views.

He offered to labor without salary, with the proviso that they permit him to work wherever the Lord might direct.

His faith began to look beyond man to God for spiritual direction as well as for physical needs. This was a forward step in his soul pilgrimage. It was a lesson in trust that the young disciple must experience before God was ready to use him. He had previously been convinced though a stranger in England he need have no anxiety for his temporal needs—"as long as I really sought to serve the Lord . . . as long as I sought the kingdom of God and his righteousness, these my temporal wants would be added unto me."

Through reading the Bible promises had been emblazoned on his memory, and these promises he believed to be sources of divine supply. In making this life-altering decision he found the following verses of special import:

"Ask, and it shall ye given you; seek, and ye shall find; knock, and it shall be opened unto you" (Matt. 7:7).

"And whatsoever ye shall ask in my name, that will I do, that the Father may be glorified in the Son. If ye shall ask anything in my name, I will do it" (John 14:13, 14).

"Therefore I say unto you, take no thought for your life, what ye shall eat, or what ye shall drink; nor yet for your body, what ye shall put on. Is not

the life more than meat, and the body than raiment?
Behold the fowls of the air: for they sow not . . . yet
your heavenly Father feedeth them. Are ye not much
better than they?" (Matt. 6: 25-26).

Strengthened by these gracious words his faith
leaped forth—he need trust no longer in man when
God had bid him come and receive.

The answer from the Society arrived late in January of 1830, stating that his connection with them was
at an end. While this door of being a missionary to
the Jews was closed, God was opening another into
which he was to step. In his twenty-fifth year he looked
out upon the world as a field of service and was willing to be led—as well as fed—by the Spirit. He remained in the South of Devon preaching wherever an
opportunity came. The Ebenezer Chapel was among
the places he visited. On New Year's day, 1831, he
attended services at the chapel where he spoke on
the difference between a *Christian* and a *happy Christian,* "and showed them whence it generally comes
that we rejoice so little in the Lord."

He was requested to bring an afternoon message,
and at its close it was suggested that he begin a series
of ten o'clock morning messages on the book of
Romans. During these morning meetings the Ebenezer
congregation asked that he become their pastor. The
group on this point was not unanimous. "Some of them
left and never returned; some left, but returned after
a while; others came to the chapel who had not been
in the habit of attending previous to my coming,"
Mr. Muller affirms.

There was no little stir in the congregation because
of the services "of this foreigner," as some of them
expressed it. Some delighted in the food for their

souls, caring little about the form, but others bitterly opposed the work of Christ. "There was," Muller writes, "in addition to this, a great stir, a spirit of enquiry, and a searching of the Scriptures. . . . And what is more than all, God set his seal upon the work in converting sinners. Twelve weeks I stood in this position, whilst the Lord graciously supplied my temporal wants, through two brethren, unasked for."

After this the whole little church, eighteen in number, extended a call for him to become their permanent pastor. The brethren were generous in their financial offer, stating the salary to be £55, or $275 a year.*

While waiting on the Lord to give His answer to the call, for he had desired to travel from place to place preaching the gospel, Muller received a new light on baptism. He was preaching at Sidmouth in April, when three ladies asked his opinion on the subject.

"I do not think that I need to be baptized again," he replied.

"But have you been baptized?" one asked.

"Yes, when I was a child."

"Have you ever read the Scriptures and prayed with reference to the subject?"

Mr. Muller had to admit that he had not.

"Then," one of them said, "I entreat you never to speak any more about it till you have done so."

This searcher after light took these remarks to heart and when he had diligently read such passages as Acts 8:36-38 and Romans 6:3-6, he said, "I saw that believers only are the proper subjects for baptism, and that immersion is the only true Scriptural mode

* An English pound in this connection represents approximately $5.00, and in this book is used on such a basis.

in which it ought to be attended to." Accordingly he was immersed.

It was during the same summer that on reading the Bible it seemed Scriptural "and according to the example of the Apostles (Acts 20:7) to break bread every Lord's day, though there is no commandment given to do so either by the Lord, or by the Holy Ghost through the apostles." From reading Ephesians 4 and Romans 12 he also reached the conclusion that there should be given a place in their meetings for brethren to speak freely, either to testify, exhort, or teach, as the Holy Spirit led them.

God was gradually leading Mr. Muller to trust the Scriptures for guidance in matters of conscience. By yielding in minor things, he found it not difficult to yield and obey in the realm of trusting God for all his supplies . . . a decision which was soon to be made.

He was about to take an important step in his life, the selection of a companion. The guidance of God in this action was sought diligently through prayer and Bible reading. Friends had told him when he first landed in England of Mr. Groves, the Exeter dentist, who had given up an excellent salary to be a missionary. In the course of his preaching he met Mary Groves, the missionary's sister, and after a short courtship, much prayer and meditation upon the matter, they were married on October 7 in a simple ceremony at the home of a friend. And for more than forty years God blessed this union.

"She was a rare woman and her price was above rubies," writes A. T. Pierson. "The heart of her husband trusted in her and the great family of orphans who were to her as children rise up even to this day to call her blessed."

Shortly before his marriage the thought of a stated salary worried Mr. Muller, for he felt that his should be a life of trust in God and not in the promise of the brethren. He found three reasons why he should give up a fixed remuneration.

1. A salary implies a fixed sum, generally made up of pew rents. But according to James 2:1-6, "pew rents are against the mind of the Lord."

2. A fixed pew rent may at times become a burden to the follower of Christ and Mr. Muller did not wish to lay the smallest straw in the way of the church's spiritual progress.

3. The whole system of pew rents and salary are liable to become a snare to the minister, in that he works for hire rather than for spiritual reasons.

At the end of October, within a month after his marriage, he announced to the Teignmouth congregation that henceforth he would receive no regular salary, and would trust wholly in the Lord for his needs. He asked that a box be placed in the chapel where whoever desired to help him might leave his offering. Henceforth he was to ask no one, "not even my beloved brethren and sisters, to help me. . . . For unconsciously I had been led to trust in an arm of flesh, going to man instead of going to the Lord at once."

Shortly afterward he and his wife were impressed with the text, "Sell that ye have and give alms," and literally were led to obey the command. "Our staff and support in this matter," he affirms when the great test came, "were Matthew 6:19-34 and John 14:13, 14. We leaned on the arm of the Lord Jesus."

From that time on never once did Mr. Muller and his wife regret taking this step. Tests of faith were soon to come, as they came throughout Muller's long Christian career-trek; but he leaned heavily on the Master's strong arm, knowing full-well that if God clothed the sparrows, fed and housed them, he would not forsake him. This was to be a walk of faith and not of sight, and the servant was to learn the lesson of trust through the school of experience.

During the first year the Lord dealt gently with his followers. Mr. Muller exults in saying, "He did not try our faith much at the commencement, but gave us first encouragement, and allowed us to see His willingness to help us before he was pleased to try it more fully." When the year closed the young minister was able to affirm that the Lord had "richly supplied all our temporal wants, though at the commencement we had no certain human prospect of a single shilling, so that . . . we have not been in the smallest degree a loser in acting according to the dictates of conscience. The Lord dealt bountifully with me, and has condescended to use me as an instrument in doing His work."

The year 1831 was to be one of testing Muller's faith, for many times there was not a single shilling left in the house, though at the proper moment faith's reward came in the form of money and supplies.

One morning when their money had been reduced to eight shillings (about $2.00, a shilling equalling approximately 25c), Muller asked the Lord for money. For four hours the preacher waited but still no reply. Then a lady came to the house.

"Do you want any money?" she asked.

Faith was tested, yet remained triumphant, and the minister replied, "I told the brethren, dear sister, when I gave up my salary, that I would for the future tell the Lord only about my wants."

"But," she replied, reaching for her purse, "He has told me to give you some money," laying in his hand two guineas.

For three days in the first of January, on the 6th, 7th and 8th, real testings came when their money was exhausted. Muller prayed faithfully, and one day the devil assaulted him severely, causing the minister almost to decide that he had gone too far in this way of trust. Then came faith's victory and the devil fled. As he returned to his room he found that a sister in the Lord had brought in about eleven dollars. "So the Lord triumphed and our faith was strengthened."

Once the minister's faith was anxious when he saw a brother open the chapel box, for he was in dire need of money. He would not ask the brother for what came in, since he often stated in the pulpit, "I desire to look neither to man nor the *box*, but to the living God." Muller resorted to prayer, asking the Lord to incline the man's heart to bring the money. Shortly the box money was given him, amounting to one pound, eight shillings and sixpence.

God was gradually leading the young minister to test His promises and see whether they were true. On February 14 there was very little money in the parsonage purse, when Muller resorted to prayer, asking God to supply. "The instant," Muller testifies, "*I got up from my knees* a brother gave me one pound . . .*"

Late in the year rent day came and there was no money to pay it. After prayer the money was sent in to cover the obligation. Concerning this incident Muller lays down a principle to which he always remained constant. "I would just observe that we never contract debts, which we believe to be unscriptural (according to Romans 13:8), and therefore we have no bills . . .

but all we buy we pay for in ready money. Thus
we always know how much we have and how much we
have a right to give away."

This was one principle upon which he was to conduct his orphanage work, and never once did he break
over from the rule of not going into debt.

God led this disciple of faith along paths of trust.
Many times there was not even bread in the parsonage
for the next meal, but in sufficient time bread arrived.
He tells of one such incident thus, "Our bread was
hardly enough for the day. . . . After dinner, when I
returned thanks, I asked him to give us our *daily
bread*, meaning literally that he would send us bread
for the evening. Whilst I was praying there was a
knock at the door of the room. After I had concluded
a poor sister came in and brought us some of her
dinner, and from another poor sister five shillings. In
the afternoon she also brought us a large loaf. Thus
the Lord not only gave us bread but also money."

Mr. Muller held that to lay up stores or hoard money
was inconsistent with a life of faith. In such cases
he thought God would send them to their hoardings
before answering their prayers. Experience confirmed
them in the conviction that a life of trust forbids
laying up treasures against unforeseen needs, since
with God *"no emergency is unforeseen and no want
unprovided for."* Hence his trust was in God and not
in his hoardings.

A third rule was greatly blessed throughout Muller's
career of trust. When money was given him for a
specific need, or purpose, he regarded it as sacred to
that trust, *and would not use or borrow it even tempo-
rarily for any other purpose.* Though reduced to dire
needs, he would not use any money set aside for

other purposes except for that specific thing. Thousands
of times in later life occasions came where such diver-
sion of funds would have provided a way out of an
emergency or tided them through a strait.

And how, you ask, did God supply his needs for
that first year of trust? Let the twenty-six-year-old
minister answer, "Now the truth is whilst . . . we have
not had even as much as a single penny left, or so
as to have the last bread on the table, and not as much
money as was needed to buy another loaf, yet never
have we had to sit down to a meal without our good
Lord having provided nourishing food for us. I am
bound to state this, and I do it with pleasure. . . . If I
had to choose this day again as to the way of living,
the Lord giving me grace, I would not choose differ-
ently."

At the end of 1831 when George summed up what
he had received in answer to prayer it amounted to
more than one hundred and thirty-one pounds, three-
fourths of which came from friends not connected with
his church. The congregation had promised their minister $275, and through a life of trust he had received
approximately $660 for the year.

"In this my freedom, I am," Mr. Muller states, "at
least able to say to myself . . . My Lord is not limited;
He can supply. . . . And thus this way of living, so
far from *leading to anxiety*, as regards possible future
want, is rather the means of *keeping from it*. . . . This
way of living has often been the means of reviving the
work of grace in my heart . . . and a fresh answer to
prayer obtained in this way has been the means of
quickening my soul and filling me with much joy."

CHAPTER IV

THE BIRTH OF A NEW IDEA

MULLER WAS ready at length for his life's work.
God had brought him from Prussia to England and
had taught him lessons in trust. Every leaning post
had been removed. This apostle of faith had laid down
those principles of trust by which his future was to
be marked. He looked entirely to God for spiritual
direction as well as for physical supplies. For what
telling he had to do, henceforth he was to seek only
the ear of God.

One thing was lacking, which God in a devious
manner was about to furnish, and that was a location
for his faith idea to germinate into a living reality.
Muller was at Teignmouth where for two and a half
years God gently taught him lessons in trust. Now
God was ready for him to begin work in Bristol.

Muller tells the turning events in a few sentences
in his "Life of Trust." "April 13. Found a letter
from Brother Craik, from Bristol. . . . He invites me
to come and help him. . . . It seems to me as if I
should shortly go, if the Lord permit."

These were short sentences, brief words, yet meaningful in the light of God's plan for Muller's future.
On the following day he wrote, "Wrote to Brother
Craik, in which I said I should come, if I clearly saw
it to be the Lord's will."

This was the bend in his life's road, and the proviso was written into the letter as well as designed
into Muller's experience . . . *if the Lord will.* Always
the minister made his plans only when God plainly
indicated that human plans and the divine will coin-
cided.

In 1829 Mr. Muller had met a kindred spirit in
Henry Craik, both being university trained men, who
had been spiritually awakened at their respective uni-
versities, Craik in Scotland and Muller in Halle.
Shortly before Muller had begun preaching on the
second coming of Christ as being in accordance with
the Scriptures, and Craik held to similar views. This
drew the two men together as kindred souls.

Due to the death of Craik's wife, he had met a
friend from Bristol who had invited him to accept
work in the city, serving as pastor of the Gideon Chapel.

A month after he had located in Bristol he wrote
to his old friend George Muller to come and help him.
For some time the young minister had felt that his
work was done at Teignmouth, though God had signally prospered him in his parish with an increase in
membership from eighteen to fifty-one. When Craik's
letter arrived he told his congregation of the invitation.

"I reminded them," he says, "of what I had told
them when they requested me to take the oversight
of them, that I could make no certain engagement,
but stay only so long with them as I should see it to
be the Lord's will to do so."

After a visit to Bristol on April 21, 1832, where
he preached at the Gideon Chapel and later at the
Pithay Chapel, Mr. Muller decided it was God's will
to leave his Teignmouth congregation. Accordingly he
and Mr. Craik laid down conditions for the new con-

gregation to accept before they would become pastors of the work.

On May 15 two letters arrived from Bristol in which the Gideon folk accepted the terms, which were, "to consider us only as ministering among them, but not in any fixed pastoral relationship, so that we may preach as we consider it to be according to the mind of God, without reference to any rules among them; that the pew-rents should be done away with, and that we should go on, respecting the supply of our temporal wants, as in Devonshire."

In less than ten days Muller and his wife moved to Bristol. At last he was in the setting for God's plan to be carried out through the simple expedient of Muller's faith. Within a month after arriving in the city God opened another station to these two preachers, Craik and Muller. The Bethesda Chapel was engaged for them, thus giving each a pulpit.

The two spiritual leaders of the congregations diligently entered upon their duties, preaching faithfully the word of redemption. When the cholera broke out that summer they visited the sick and risked their lives to care for the dying. "Who may be next, God alone knows," wrote Mr. Muller, displaying the dreadful tension which existed as the scourge raged. "I have never realized so much the nearness of death. . . . Just now, ten in the evening, the funeral bell is ringing, and has been ringing the greater part of the evening. It rings almost all the day. Into thine hands, O Lord, I commend myself."

Through that dreadful summer the blessings of God were signally upon the two chapel groups. On January 4, 1833, the congregations were slightly disturbed at the thought of losing their pastors. For on that day

Muller and Craik received a letter from Bagdad inviting them to go there as missionaries. Enclosed in the letter of invitation was a draft for $1,000 to cover their traveling expenses. But the glory of the Lord had been so blessed upon their chapel services that the pastors decided to remain at their Bristol posts of duty.

"The meetings for enquirers were so largely attended that, though they sometimes lasted for more than four hours, it was frequently the case that many . . . had to be sent away for lack of time and strength on the part of the two workers," declares Mr. Muller.

For eight years the Gideon Chapel, jointly with the Bethesda Chapel, was the scene of their spiritual ministrations.

At the close of 1833 Muller took stock of God's dealings with him since he had begun to live by faith alone in the promises of God. He found that his income for this time was approximately $3,700, whereas his stated salary for the same length of time would have been only about $900.

"During the last three years," he affirms in reviewing his income through faith, "I never have asked anyone for anything; but, by the help of the Lord, I have been enabled at all times to bring my wants to Him, and He graciously supplied them all."

The previous year Mr. Muller had been given a copy of August H. Franke's life, and as time permitted he read it through. The inspiration of Franke proved a great boon to Muller's faith, for it showed him that God for thirty years during Franke's life had been able to supply all the needs for nearly 2,000 orphans, and that for a hundred years the noble work had been continued through faith.

Muller was touched by the condition of the orphans and street gamins round about him, and he decided as inspired by Franke's work to gather them around him for instruction. At eight o'clock in the morning he gathered the children from the street to his home, fed them a little breakfast, and then for an hour and a half taught them out of the Scriptures. The work increased on his hands until it included older folk as well.

He found himself feeding from thirty to forty such persons, and as the number increased the Lord's provisions also increased. One kept pace with the other.

"God had planted a seed in the soil of Mr. Muller's heart, presently to spring up in the orphan work," writes A. T. Pierson. While the plan was not then carried to fruition, still the central thought was not lost sight of. "This thought ultimately," declares the apostle of faith, "issued in the formation of the Scriptural Knowledge Institution and in the establishment of the Orphan Houses."

Doubtless February 21, 1834, was the crowning day up to that time of God's dealings with George Muller. "I was led this morning to form a plan for the establishing, upon Scriptural principles, of an institution for the spread of the gospel at home and abroad. I trust this matter is of God . . ."

Several reasons prompted this action. Other societies, he held, were formed on the assumption that the world would gradually become better and better, "and at last the whole world will be converted." This belief he held to be contrary to the Bible and hence could not endorse it.

The worldly connection of other societies was contrary to God's Word. "The connection with the world is too marked in these religious societies, for every one who pays a guinea . . . is considered a member . . . and has a right to vote."

Other societies asked the unconverted for money, which was contrary to Mr. Muller's principles. The leaders in such societies were ofttimes wealthy, but unregenerate, individuals without a true knowledge of God. A final reason for not believing in existing organizations was that they contracted debts, which long ago God had taught him to be unworthy of a trustful life.

"It appeared to us to be his will," Muller explains, "that we should be entirely separate from these socie- ties . . ."

Accordingly on the evening of March 5, 1834, a public meeting was held where "The Scriptural Knowl- edge Institution for Home and Abroad" was formed. The founding of the Institution was accompanied by a statement of principles and objects, which in sub- stance are as follows:

The principles were stated thus:

1. "We consider every believer bound . . . to help the cause of Christ."

2. "We never intend to ask unconverted persons of rank or wealth to countenance this institution. . . . In the name of God we set up our banners."

3. "We do not mean to ask unbelievers for money."

4. "We reject altogether the help of unbelievers in managing . . . the affairs of the Institution."

5. "We intend never to enlarge the field of labor by contracting debts . . . but in secret prayer . . . we shall carry the wants of the Institution to the Lord, and act according to the means that God shall give us."

6. "We do not reckon the success of the Institution

by the amount of money given . . . but by the Lord's blessing upon the work."

7. "We desire to go simply according to the Scripture, without compromising the truth."

The objects of the Institution were:

1. To assist day schools, Sunday schools. "We consider it unscriptural that any person who does not profess to know the Lord themselves should be allowed to give religious instruction." "The Institution does not assist any adult school . . . except the teachers are believers."

2. To circulate the Holy Scriptures.

3. To aid missionary efforts. "We desire to assist those missionaries whose proceedings appear to be most according to the Scriptures."

This indeed is a large order for an institution whose founder wrote two days later, *"Today we have only one shilling left"* — only one shilling between two preachers and their families. There were no patrons, no committees, and no membership. There was to be no asking for funds, and the responsibility rested solely upon the frail efforts of two ministers, both of whom were decidedly poor!

The worldly outlook was small indeed. But Muller had mastered the lesson on outlooks—for he lived by the heavenly *up*look, and not the earthly *out*look!

Whatever might have been thought of the Institution in its beginning, and its principles of organization, it has continued operation upon the same plan for more than a hundred years with God as its sole patron and prayer as its only appeal. Its world-wide work has been signally blessed and prospered.

God had found a man he could trust and used him as His instrument in giving birth to this work. Muller was missionary spirited, for during his earlier years he had tried to become officially connected with some missionary endeavor. He had learned to take counsel and direction entirely from God. He had discovered the power for spiritual enduement which lies in Bible reading, and had filled his soul with God's Word so that he might test his daily walk by these principles which God had inspired.

Another source of his spiritual strength was found in cutting loose from worldly attachments. He would not even as much as give money to a school or a Sunday school where the teachers were not believers, nor would he ask for money from anyone, let alone the fact that he would not list wealthy patrons as promoters of his work. He had renounced self, the world and its attachments, that he might give himself to secret prayer. Out of such endeavors flowed the stream of his power with God.

With God as its Patron, prayer as its appeal, believing workers at its head, the Institution could but flourish.

During the first seven months money began to flow in so that active work was undertaken. Almost a hundred and sixty-eight pounds were contributed by various persons, which was carefully expended to promote the objects of the work. During this time in the Sunday school 120 children received instruction; 40 in the Adult school; 209 children were taught in the four Day schools, two for boys and two for girls, 54 of this number being free pupils and the others paying part of their expenses.

The work of Bible distribution, always a large object for promotion, began at once. During the initial seven months 482 Bibles and 520 New Testaments were circulated while $285 was given to aid missionary activities.

On January 21, 1835, Mr. Muller entered in his Journal these words, "Received in answer to prayer from an unexpected quarter, five pounds for the Scriptural Knowledge Institution. *The Lord pours in, whilst we seek to pour out.*" This was always his plan of operation. He sought God to pour in the supplies, and he diligently furnished sources through which they might be distributed. As long as Muller saw to the careful distribution of money and supplies, God never failed in pouring in the needed materials.

He had struck a partnership with God, and had promised to dispense whatever the Almighty provided. The partnership remained constant to the end.

Working so diligently in promoting the Institution whose object was to reach the unconverted abroad as well as at home, Mr. Muller often in those early years felt a pull on his heart toward foreign missionary service. On January 28, he entered in his Journal, "I have . . . prayed much to ascertain whether the Lord will have me to go as a missionary to the East Indies, and I am most willing to go . . ." The following day he wrote, "I have been greatly stirred up to pray about going to Calcutta as a missionary. May the Lord guide me in this matter."

Forty-two years later he said about those early missionary longings, "After all my repeated and earnest prayer in the commencement of 1835, and willingness on my part to go, if it were the Lord's will, still He did not send me."

During those forty-two years and the subsequent twenty-one years until his death, Mr. Muller accomplished more for missions by remaining in England

and by praying in funds than had he gone to some of the many mission fields to which his heart was drawn. God knew he would do more by *praying* than *going*, so he kept him in Bristol, from which emanated streams of influence and spiritual power felt around the world.

From the birth of this idea—the founding of the Institution—during Muller's lifetime more than seven and a half million dollars were to be poured into the coffers of the work, through this man's prayer.

And never from the beginning until the present day, now more than forty-two years after Mr. Muller's death, has a single person been asked to contribute. God still remains the Institution's sole Patron, as He was during the years of the apostle of faith's earthly ministry.

There were greater things ahead in this thirty-year-old minister's life, which should branch from the work already started. Muller was to be God's friend of the homeless waifs, and God was but seasoning him for his enlarged battle of faith. The idea was already at work in George's soul; he was but waiting the full knowledge that *now is God's time*.

For when God's moment arrived, Muller was never a moment late.

CHAPTER V

INTO HIS LIFE'S WORK AT LAST

GRADUALLY GOD'S providence led Mr. Muller to the sphere of his life's work. Now at Bristol, after the young minister's soul had been strengthened by eighteen months of trust for the success of the Institution, God was ready to thrust him forth into his real mission. Other activities were but preparatory to the orphanage work. God had at length through the devious paths of providence faith-energized a man to whom He could trust this important activity.

For months Mr. Muller had been thinking about founding an orphanage. He had prayed about it often, and his classes for destitute children and older folks gradually led him to the decision that God's time had finally arrived.

On November 20, 1835, he found at a sister's house a life of Franke which touched the well-springs of his ambition. He wrote, "I have frequently, for a long time, thought of laboring in a similar way." The following day he entered in his Journal, "Today I have had it very much impressed on my heart no longer merely to *think* about the establishment of an orphan house, but actually to set about it. I have been very much in prayer regarding it . . . to ascertain the Lord's mind."

These were the soul-beginnings of the ambition plan.

On December 2 he was to take the first outward and
formal step toward bringing into reality this prayer-
dream. He says, "Therefore, I have this day taken the
first actual step in the matter, in having ordered bills
to be printed, announcing a public meeting on December 9, at which I intend to lay before the brethren
my thoughts concerning the orphan house . . ."

Mr. Muller was not to wait for the brethren's opinion,
advice or first-fruits of meager gifts. For on December
5 while reading the Bible at his evening prayer season,
the Scriptures blazed forth in a text which inspired
his faith to immediate action.

"This evening," he affirms, "I was struck in reading
the Scriptures with these words, *'Open thy mouth wide,
and I will fill it.'* I was led to apply this scripture to
the orphan house, and ask the Lord for premises, one
thousand pounds and suitable individuals to take care
of the children." His faith flamed forth when God
spoke.

From that moment this text formed one of his life
mottoes, and the promise became a power in molding
his future work. The text was his check on heaven's
bank, and cashable for any needed amount, so Muller's
faith attested.

God's seal on the work was not long in coming, for
his faith obtained the substance in the form of a gift,
the first of many thousands. Muller's diary entry is
short, but meaningful, "Today I received the first
shilling for the orphan house." This was only two days
after his memorable outreach of faith for the orphanage.

On the afternoon of the meeting, December 9, came
the first gift of furniture in form of a large wardrobe.
Concerning that night meeting, more or less a form
since God had put his sanction upon the work and gifts

had already been coming in through Muller's faith, the faith-venturing preacher says, "As soon as I began to speak at the meeting I received peculiar assistance from God. After the meeting ten shillings were given me. There was purposely no collection. . . . After the meeting a sister offered herself for the work. I went home, happy in the Lord and full of confidence that the matter would come to pass."

The following morning a statement of the meeting was given to the press. Immediate response burst forth following the news article, and gifts began to come in, as well as offers of life services of the givers themselves.

On December 10 Muller received a letter, one of the many scores which were to follow during his long orphanage career, "We propose ourselves for the service of the intended orphan house, if you think us qualified for it; also to give up all the furniture, etc., which the Lord has given us, for its use; and to do this without receiving any salary whatever; believing that, if it be the will of the Lord to employ us, He will supply all our needs."

Since that day there has never been a lack of competent, cheerful and devoted helpers, though the work rapidly extended beyond Muller's strongest dreams.

In the evening of the same day, as tokens from the Lord, individuals sent in "three dishes, twenty-eight plates, three basins, one jug, four mugs, three saltstands, one grater, four knives and five forks." On December 12 came more dishes and fifty pounds for the work. On the thirteenth came twenty-nine yards of print, "also a sister offered herself for the work." Mr. Muller reported one gift with the same calm and equipoise as the other.

On the next day came eight shillings and "a brother

and sister offered themselves." Still there were no surprise remarks from the apostle of trust, for he had believed that God would *fill his open mouth,* and in this filling all came as from God. Similar gifts continued daily.

Came basins and mugs and dessert spoons, a skimmer, a toasting fork and a dredge, also pillow cases and table cloths, as well as "fifty-five yards of sheeting, and twelve yards of calico."

The orphanage was on its way . . . for the bounteous hand of God was overflowing with gifts.

On December 17 Mr. Muller turned down the gift of $500 from a poor woman, thinking that she was unable to give so much. She was weak in body and her weekly earnings were less than a dollar.

"But," she replied in triumphant faith, "the Lord Jesus has given His last drop for me, and should I not give Him this hundred pounds?"

The gift Mr. Muller discovered had come through the death of the girl's grandmother, and he accepted it with gratitude to God for using "this poor, sickly sister as an instrument in so considerable gift, for helping at its very commencement the work."

At last Mr. Muller was able to set a definite date for opening an orphans' house for girls. As funds came in he secured a large house, No. 6 North Wilson Street, where he had been living for some time, by renting it for one year. April 1, 1836, was set as the formal opening day. He informed the public that he would receive applications for entrance, and shortly after he intimated that a second house would be opened to receive small children, both boys and girls.

During the weeks that Mr. Muller had prayed in the materials for the house, the funds for the rent and its equipment, the laborers to carry on the work, he had forgotten to pray for orphans. *And on the opening day not one applicant was received!*

He had taken it for granted that the children would come. He spent two hours at the house waiting for applicants, and then dejectedly walked home. On his way this thought rushed to his mind, "I have prayed about everything connected with this work—for money, for a house, for helpers, about the various articles of furniture, etc., but I have never asked the Lord to send me orphans."

That night he laid low in prayer, prevailing with God to send children for the home. Faith once more gained a divine audience, for the *very next day* he received the first application for entrance. Within a month forty-two children were seeking admission, with twenty-six already in the home and more arriving daily.

Throughout the year there were to be testings of personal faith, but God never failed him. As a sample of such trials on November 30 he writes, "Being in great need, I was led, yesterday morning, earnestly to ask the Lord; and in answer to this petition a brother gave me, last evening, ten pounds." Morning prayer was answered by the evening gift.

Mr. Muller testifies that in his lifetime fifty thousand such specific prayers were answered. Years before he died, about the middle of his career, he affirmed that up to that time five thousand of his definite prayers had been answered on the day of asking.

He made it a habit to keep a notebook with two page entries. On one page he gave the petition and the date, and on the opposite page he entered the date of the answer. In this manner he was able to keep record of definite petitions, and their specific answers. He recom-

mended this form to believers who desired specific results to their prayers. Thus there is no guesswork as
to when God answers prayers.

At the beginning of 1836 Mr. Muller had asked for
a thousand pounds and an orphanage house along with
its equipment. In reviewing that year's work, he found
that God had given him his first orphanage house on
Wilson Street, and seven months after the opening of
the first house he obtained another one located at No. 1
Wilson Street. This received its first children on November 18. A review of his financial returns showed
gifts for the orphanages of seven hundred and seventy
pounds, and he himself had received for his personal
needs two hundred and thirty-two pounds.

During that year, God furnished more than the $5,000
asked as the initial starter of the work. Closing the first
orphanage year, he relates, "On December 31, we had
this evening a prayer meeting to praise the Lord for
His goodness during the past year, and to ask Him for
a continuance of His favors."

The blessings of God were so numerous that by April
8, 1837, there were thirty orphans in each house, No. 6
Wilson Street caring for older girls and No. 1 giving
a home to young boys and girls.

The founder of this work, asking at first for a hundred pounds, affirms that in his own mind the thing
was as good as done, and he often thanked God for the
sum as though already in hand. When about to print
his "Narrative of the Lord's Dealings," he took it in
mind to ask God for the total sum, not counting what
had come in for his own needs, before the book issued
from the press.

"He therefore gave himself anew to prayer; and on
June 15th the whole sum was complete . . ." writes Mr.

Pierson. No appeal was made to the public, God alone receiving his petitions daily for eighteen months and ten days.

It was in the year 1837 that Mr. Muller, then thirty-two, felt a deep conviction that his own growth in grace and power for service were indispensable for the promotion of the work. He sought two things; first more retirement for secret prayer and communion with God and provision for the spiritual oversight of the church, the total number of communicants being at this time nearly four hundred. He found himself too busy to pray as he ought.

After learning the lesson of being busy in the work of the Lord, too busy in fact to pray, he told his brethren that four hours of work after an hour of prayer would accomplish more than five hours without prayer. This rule henceforth he faithfully kept.

Considering the fact that there were now two distinct churches to be looked after, and also two orphanage houses, there was a meeting in October of that year where the two congregations decided to unite into one, to lessen the separate meetings conducted each week.

On October 21 another house was secured in Wilson Street which was opened to receive orphan boys. Mr. Muller now had under his care ninety-six orphans. His prayer for premises, suitable helpers and the thousand pounds were abundantly answered.

He remarks, "When I was asking the petition I was fully aware what I was doing, *i.e.* asking for something that I had *no natural prospect of getting from the brethren I knew,* but which was not too much for the Lord to grant."

In reviewing the year 1837, Muller states, "Ninety, therefore, daily sit down to table. Lord, look on the necessities of thy servant"—a prayer which God abundantly answered. Not once during the year was a single meal unsupplied. Throughout all his experience in conducting the orphanages this servant of God testifies that no meal, even when he was feeding two thousand orphans daily by faith, was more than thirty minutes late.

At the opening of the boys' house Mr. Muller received his first legacy, which was from a little boy who saved some funds during his fatal illness. Knowing that he was soon to die, the lad asked that his savings, amounting to a little more than $1.50, be sent to Mr. Muller. The minister took it as his first legacy, and though small in amount, he believed that God was peculiarly placing his approval upon the new venture of the boys' house.

Many asked Mr. Muller how he sought to know the will of God, in that nothing was undertaken, not even the smallest expenditure, without feeling certain he was in God's will. In the following words he gave his answer:

"1. I seek at the beginning to *get my heart into such a state that it has no will of its own in regard to a given matter*. Nine-tenths of the difficulties are overcome when our hearts are ready to do the Lord's will, whatever it may be. When one is truly in this state, it is usually but a little way to the knowledge of what His will is.

"2. Having done this, *I do not leave the result to feeling or simple impressions*. If so, I make myself liable to great delusions.

"3. I seek the will of the Spirit of God through or in connection with the Word of God. The Spirit and the Word must be combined. If I look to the Spirit alone without the Word, I lay myself open to great delusions also.

"4. *Next I take into account providential circum-*

stances. These plainly indicate God's will in connection with His Word and Spirit.

"5. *I ask God in prayer to reveal His will to me aright.*

"6. *Thus through prayer to God, the study of the Word and reflection,* I come to a deliberate judgment according to the best of my ability and knowledge, and if my mind is thus at peace, and continues so after two or three more petitions, I proceed accordingly. In trivial matters and in transactions involving most important issues, I have found this method always effective."

And did this plan work? one asks. Let Mr. Muller's testimony answer.

"I never remember," he wrote three years before his death, "in all my Christian course, a period now (in March, 1895) of sixty-nine years and four months, that I ever SINCERELY AND PATIENTLY sought to know the will of God by *the teaching of the Holy Ghost*, through *the instrumentality of the Word of God*, but I have been ALWAYS directed rightly. But if *honesty of heart* and *uprightness before God* were lacking, or if I did not *patiently* wait upon God for instruction, or if I preferred *the counsel of my fellow men* to the declarations of *the Word of the living God*, I made great mistakes." (Italics his.)

When asked why he undertook the work of the Institution, Mr. Muller replied, "The first and primary object of the Institution was, and still is, that God might be magnified by the fact that the Orphans under my care were, and are, provided with all they need only by *prayer* and *faith*, without anyone being asked by me or my fellow-laborers, whereby it might be seen that God is FAITHFUL STILL AND HEARS PRAYER STILL."

Chapter VI

TRUSTING GOD FOR DAILY SUPPLIES

During the next seven years Mr. Muller's problem was one of trusting for daily supplies. There were three houses to be maintained, and about a hundred orphans to be clothed and fed. The daily expenditure was heavy, the rent considerable, and the personal needs of his helpers were great. In addition to this, the work of the Institution, assisting schools, paying teachers, running Sunday schools and helping missionaries demanded a constant stream of money flowing in.

Early in 1838 sickness fell heavily upon the leader, and as his custom he went to his knees in the midst of his affliction. While reading the Bible his eyes fell upon the 68th Psalm and in the course of his meditation, the words "A father of the fatherless" stood out in mighty letters as a divine promise in this stressful hour.

"This word, 'A father of the fatherless' " he affirms, "contains enough encouragement to cast thousands of orphans, with all their needs, upon the loving heart of God."

From then on the burdens were not his but the Lord's. He cast them from his shoulders through loving trust upon the broad arms of the Master. During June God tested his faith by suddenly shutting off the gifts which had so abundantly flowed in. Muller took the matter to the Lord.

He enters in his Journal under date of July 22 (1838), "This evening I was walking in our little garden . . . meditating on Hebrews 13:8, 'Jesus Christ the same yesterday, and today, and forever.' . . . All at once the present need of the Orphan-House was brought to my mind. Immediately I was led to say to myself, Jesus in His love and power has hitherto supplied me with what I have needed for the Orphans, and in the same unchangeable love and power He will provide with what I may need for the future. A flow of joy came into my soul . . ."

This soul joy was the fore announcer of a coming blessing. "About one minute later a letter was brought to me, enclosing a bill for twenty pounds," he writes.

In this case God's timing was perfect, for when the need existed, and Muller had prayed, the next moment the supply was forthcoming.

Throughout that turbulent year Mr. Muller's faith was sorely tried, for often there was not a single penny in the houses; but God was leading him forth, proving and testing him in the smaller things, so that later he might be able to feed as many as two thousand children daily through the instrument of prayer.

On September 18 the funds were exhausted, and Mr. Muller thought of selling the things that could be done without in the homes. "This morning," he writes, "I had asked the Lord, if it might be, to prevent the necessity of our doing so."

That afternoon a lady from London, who had been staying in Bristol, brought a package with money in it from her daughter who had sent it several days before.

"That the money had been so near," declares Mr. Muller, "for several days without being given, is a plain proof that it was in the heart of God to help us; but because He delights in the prayers of His children, He had allowed us to pray so long . . . to try our faith and to make the answer so much the sweeter."

During this time Mr. Muller's health was not good and his friends asked him to go away for a rest, but he refused, saying, "I must remain to pass with my dear Orphans through the trial, though these dear ones know nothing about it, because their tables are as well supplied as when there was eight hundred pounds in the bank; and they have lack of nothing."

Many times he was forced to say, "The funds are exhausted." But not once did these words hold true over night. Funds might have been depleted during the day, at times all day, again for hours, but when nightfall came there was something on hand for the next day. With this faith apostle, this meant daily trusting for *today's* needs.

It was during these direful days that Muller declared, "Long before the trials came, I had more than once stated publicly that answers to prayer in the time of need — the manifestation of the hand of God stretched out for our help — were just the very ends for which the Institution was established."

Sometimes in plenty, but oftener in poverty, his faith carried the orphanages on. Many times in dire straits the money would arrive at the very moment of prayer, or as he was reading the list of needs for the day. His trust in "the father of the fatherless" was so confident that not once did he turn a child away.

Under date of August 8, 1839, he affirms, "Though

there is no money in hand, yet are we so little discouraged that we have received today one orphan boy, and have given notice for the admission of six other children, which will bring the number up to 98 altogether."

Often gifts came in at the very *instant of prayer*. On March 5, 1839, he writes, *"Whilst I was in prayer, Q. Q. sent a check for seven pounds . . ."*

Closing the report for the year 1839, he sums up the bounteous blessing of God, saying, "For the Orphan Houses, *without any one having been asked* by us, the sum of £3,067 8s. 9¼d. has been given *entirely* as the result of prayer to God, from the commencement of the work to December 9, 1839."

The following year was started without enough money to carry through the first day. A peculiar incident occurred that day which showed Mr. Muller's character. After the usual Watch night service, about an hour past midnight, a friend, whom Mr. Muller knew to be in debt, handed him a sealed envelope with money in it. "I resolved, therefore, without opening the paper to return it. . . . This was done *when I knew there was not enough in hand to meet the expenses of the day."*

Seven hours later, "about eight this morning," a brother brought five pounds for the orphans. "Observe, the brother is led to bring it *at once."* God honored Mr. Muller's faith in giving back the money he knew the lady needed to pay her debts more than the orphans needed it.

On January 12, 1841, after he had been forced to delay printing his yearly report because of a lack of funds, he notes that the Lord supplies this need and in addition $5,000 was received for missionary work in the East Indies. Here is his prayer testimony concerning this the largest gift he had thus far received, "In all my experience I have found . . . that if I could only settle a certain thing to be done was according to the will of God, that means were soon obtained to carry it into effect."

God never failed His servant. Often he was led through the valley of great want, but always to the shining peak of supply. God's dealings were generous. One day in 1841 when Mr. Muller had taken only a shilling from the house box, a lady came with twopence, saying, "It is but a trifle, but I must give it." It so happened that one of the pennies was needed to make up the amount of money necessary to buy bread!

A week later a single penny was needed to fill out the dinner menu . . . but no penny was in hand. When the Girls' box was opened out rolled one penny. "Even the gift of a penny," states Muller, "was thus evidently under the ordering of our kind Father."

At the close of the year, he affirmed, "We are now brought to the close of the sixth year of this . . . work (December 9), having in hand only the money which has been put by for the rent; but during the whole of this year we have been supplied with all that was needed."

During the next three years Mr. Muller literally fed the orphans out of God's hand. The supply was almost like that of the manna in that it was to be gathered each day afresh. There was scarcely anything left over from one day to another. Often money had to be prayed in before breakfast could be eaten or the evening meal finished.

But Mr. Muller's faith was so dominant that however much the need, he rested calmly in the divine assurance that God's hand would contain a bounteous supply when the moment arrived. He and worry parted forever. Though he was deeply concerned, he never fretted at delay in receiving answers to his requests.

On February 15, 1842, his attitude is typical. "I sat peacefully down to give myself to meditation over the Word, considering that was now my service, though I knew not whether there was a morsel of bread for tea in any one of the houses, *but being assured that the Lord would provide.* For through grace my mind is so fully assured of the faithfulness of the Lord, that in the midst of the greatest need, I am enabled in peace to go about my other work. Indeed, did not the Lord give me this, which is the result of trusting in Him, I should be scarcely able to work at all."

His mind was fixed in God and would not be moved, for he knew at the proper time the money or the food would arrive.

March 19 began in poverty and dire need, only seven shillings having come in during three days. "There was not one ray of light as far as natural prospects." So Mr. Muller proposed to his workers that the day be set for prayer. When they met at ten-thirty, immediately by three separate people twenty-one shillings were brought in. They called a similar session of prayer for the evening, for there were yet three shillings lacking. Before the evening service was over the three shillings had arrived, plus an additional three.

Week by week God led Muller into deeper lessons of trust, always closing the day's trust sessions with a speedy answer. On April 12, he affirms, "We were never in greater need than today, perhaps never in so much, when I received this morning one hundred pounds from the East Indies. My prayer had been again this morning particularly that our Father would pity us, and now at last send *larger sums.* I was not in the least surprised or excited when this donation came, for I took it as that *which came in answer to prayer and had been long looked for.*"

During these testing days Mr. Muller was often asked how he managed to build such a strong faith in God. He replied that he endeavored to keep his faith in God strong not only for daily supplies of food for the orphans and money for the missionary work but also for the spiritual concern of the world.

"Let not Satan deceive you," writes Mr. Muller during those faith-wrenching days, "in making you think you could not have the same faith, but that it is only for persons situated as I am. When I lose such a thing as a key, I ask the Lord to direct me to it, and I look for an answer to my prayer; when a person with whom I have an appointment does not come . . . I ask the Lord to be pleased to hasten him to me, and I look for an answer. . . . Thus in all my temporal and spiritual concerns I pray to the Lord and expect an answer to my requests; and may not you do the same, dear believing reader?"

In giving advice gained through daily trials of his faith, this father of the orphans laid down rules for Christians to follow by which they might also strengthen their faith. These rules are:

"1. Read the Bible and meditate upon it. God has become known to us through prayer and meditation upon His own Word.

"2. Seek to maintain an upright heart and a good conscience.

"3. If we desire our faith to be strengthened, we should not shrink from opportunities where our faith may be tried, and therefore, through trial, be strengthened.

"The last important point for the strengthening of our faith is that we let God work for us, when the hour of trial of our faith comes, and do not work a deliverance of our own."

"Would the believer therefore have his faith strengthened, he must *give God time to work*," he declares.

The year 1843, as the previous, was one of trials and triumphs of faith. In June there was no money, but before each day was over prayer supplied the lack. In December came mighty loads upon Mr. Muller's heart. He exercised faith and proclaimed that the work undertaken was not particularly to feed the orphans, as great as this was, nor for their spiritual welfare as glorious and blessed as this is.

"The primary object of the work is," he observed, "to show before the whole world . . . that even in these last evil days the living God is ready to prove Himself as the living God, by being ever willing to help . . . and answer the prayers of those who trust in Him."

Attesting the glorious supply which he daily obtained from God's hand, he says, "The narrative of the events of these days is imperfect. *The way in which the Lord stretched out His hand day to day, and from meal to meal, cannot be accurately described.*"

Even his own personal needs were supplied by the Lord on this "each day for itself" basis.

For one hundred and thirty-four days he daily asked the Lord to send a gift a lady had promised in 1842. The answer came on March 8, 1843. He affirms, "Day after day now has passed away and the money did not come . . . whilst day by day I brought my petition before the Lord that He would bless this sister. . . . At last, on the one hundred and thirty-fourth day since I daily besought the Lord about this matter . . . I received a letter from the sister, informing me that the five hundred pounds had been paid into the hands of my bankers."

This *day by day* experience of eating from God's outstretched hand was slowly leading up to a turning point in Mr. Muller's career. God had far grander accomplishments in store for him than merely feeding a hundred orphans. At first God wanted to know whether his servant would be faithful to his prayer trust in these smaller matters before leading him forth to the greater work.

This new turn in affairs began on March 31, 1843, when Muller called at the Houses to make arrangements for the day, and a worker told him that a Miss G—, who occupied house No. 4 on Wilson Street, had informed her that they wished to give up their house, and if possible wanted Mr. Muller to take it for another orphan House.

"When I came home," Mr. Muller informs us, "this matter greatly occupied my mind. I could not but ask the Lord again and again whether He would have me to open another Orphan House, and whether the time was now come that I should serve Him still more extensively in this matter."

He reviewed the situation carefully, finding that there were more applications for admission than he had room to care for, and that fifteen of the children in the Infant House were old enough to be promoted to the Girls' House. Until this time there had been no other house on Wilson Street, near the present places occupied, for rent. There were also two sisters who would take care of the new house if and when opened.

In the bank was three hundred pounds of the recent large gift which could be used to furnish the new house.

Surveying these conditions, he turned to the Spirit for leadings. "I therefore gave myself to prayer. I prayed day after day, *without saying anything to any human being*. I prayed two and twenty days without mentioning it to my dear wife. On that day on which I had come to the conclusion . . . to establish another Orphan House, I received fifty pounds from A.B. What a striking confirmation that the Lord would help though the necessities should increase more and more."

He realized what this added burden would mean. For five years he had trusted each day for its supplies, and the new house would only increase this load on his faith life. In spite of this his belief in God commanded a forward march, for Muller never tired of *"this precious way of depending upon the Lord from day to day."*

While he was praying about the new house, a lady from Germany, recently blessed by his work, asked him to visit that country. She felt his influence would be a benediction to his native land. But it seemed unwise for Mr. Muller to leave at the time, and besides, it would require many hundreds of pounds to leave with the overseers for the orphans, as well as to finance his trip. Moreover, he desired to publish a German edition of his life story, "A Narrative of Some of the Lord's Dealings with Mr. George Muller."

The publication alone would take between a hundred and two hundred pounds. Yet he realized however great the obstacles, if it be the Lord's will, he

would go. "I could not but pray about it," he informs us. "I could not but feel drawn to go to Germany in love of the Lord and in pity towards the
poor Church of Christ in that country." He remembered the few truly converted ministers to be found
there and in Prussia when he was a young man. His
faith began to prevail.

"I had a secret satisfaction," he writes, "in the
greatness of the difficulties. . . . So far from being
cast down on account of them, they delighted my soul.
. . . I did nothing but pray. Prayer and faith . . .
helped me over the difficulties."

From the human standpoint there was little prospect
of receiving the necessary funds, but leaving the matter
to the Lord, he was overwhelmed with a peaceful
calm. ". . . my soul is at peace. The Lord's time is
not yet come; but when it is come He will blow away
all these obstacles."

Less than fifteen minutes after he had prayed on
July 12, God sent in seven hundred and two pounds,
three shillings and seven pence. Early in August, after
fifty days of waiting on the Lord, he and his wife
were on their way to Germany.

While in Stuttgart, Mr. Muller labored to reform
the Strict Baptist Church in the city, but met with
severe opposition. While the visit seemed a failure,
however, it was checkered with a blessing. For he
was enabled while there to translate the "Narrative"
into German and 4,000 copies came from the press
before he sailed for Bristol in February, 1844.

After a second German trip, where he reëstablished
the work of faith begun in Stuttgart, he returned to
England to begin anew his prayer quest for funds
to open the fourth orphan house. When he was ready

to take the house offered him on Wilson Street, a difficulty arose which caused him to examine carefully God's will in the matter.

Before going on his first German trip he felt certain that God was opening the way for the house to be operated. For nearly ten years he had rented houses for his orphans, and "had never had any desire to build an Orphan House. On the contrary, I decidedly preferred spending the means which might come in for present necessities, and desired rather to enlarge the work according to the means the Lord might be pleased to give. Thus it was till the end of October, 1845, when I was led to consider this matter in a light in which I had never done before."

God was preparing to thrust him forth in another faith adventure which would surpass even his most extended dreams. God had been carefully schooling him in trust lessons, and now that he had learned how to believe for daily supplies, and for months had literally been fed meal by meal from God's hand, the Father of the fatherless was to open a new and untried door for him.

Mr. Muller was willing to step into any door the Master would set ajar.

The matter climaxed in a decidedly unusual manner on October 31, 1845. When he was about to rent the vacated house near his other properties, a man wrote stating that the orphan houses were a detriment to the neighboring house owners. He was courteous and kindly in his remarks, but firm nevertheless. The man felt that in various ways the neighbors were inconvenienced by the Orphan Houses on Wilson Street. He left the matter to Mr. Muller's wise judgment.

This was a new item which Muller's faith had not

previously faced. He did, however, want to live peacefully with his neighbors, so he took the request to
prayer. Carefully he weighed the *pro* and *con* arguments for moving from Wilson Street. To move, he
knew, meant to build, and up until this time he had
not thought it God's will to take this step of faith.
But God's time was about to arrive and Mr. Muller
had learned to step when God's hour struck, however
massive the problem or vexing the difficulty.

Chapter VII

BUILDING FOR GOD AND ORPHANS

GOD'S HOUR had finally arrived when Mr. Muller should step out on the divine promises and build. After weighing the complaint in the letter against the orphanage, on November 3, 1845, he laid the matter before the Lord.

This was a memorable occasion and concerning it he writes, "After I had spent a few hours in prayer . . . I began to see that the Lord would lead me to build, and that His intentions were not only to benefit the orphans . . . but also the bearing of further testimony that He could and would provide large sums . . . and that He would enlarge the work, so that if I once did build a house, it might be large enough to accommodate three hundred orphans."

The following day he and his wife proposed to meet morning by morning and pray about the building. "We continued meeting for prayer," he says, "morning by morning for fifteen days, but not a single donation came; yet my heart was not discouraged. The more I prayed, the more I was assured that the Lord would give the means."

On December 9, thirty-five days had passed, "whilst I was day by day waiting upon God for means for this work, and not a single penny had been given to me.

Nevertheless this did not in the least discourage me, but my assurance . . . increased more and more."

This was the day that God gave him the text, "Let patience have her perfect work, that ye may be perfect and entire, wanting nothing."

After having this text hung on the walls of his memory, he asked God to increase his faith and to sustain his patience. The following day came God's answer in the form of the largest donation he had received up to that time. It was a thousand pounds from a friend.

"When I received it I was as calm, as quiet as if I had only received one shilling," Mr. Muller tells us.

With this seal of God upon the work, his faith took a new grip upon the promises, and henceforth it was but a matter of waiting upon the Lord to send the funds. December 13 brought another gift more important than the first in the form of the free services of a Christian architect, who offered to draw the plans and superintend the building without payment. This was another proof that the Lord was directing Mr. Muller's prayers and intentions toward building.

Slowly the funds began to come in, though Mr. Muller had made no public announcement of his plan to build. He did not overlook the fact that if it required faith to care for a hundred and thirty children, which were then in the home, it would take greater faith to feed and clothe 300.

After the sixty-fifth day of prayer God sent a gift of fifty pounds, which was soon followed by another thousand-pound donation.

On January 31, 1846, Muller went to see a piece of land that seemed available for the building. This was the eighty-ninth day since he had begun to call upon

God for a building, and he thought God would soon furnish suited grounds. He wanted about seven acres close to Bristol. God had the land which in due time, after a testing of faith, would be provided.

"Feb. 3. Saw the land . . ." he entered in his diary. The following day he began negotiations for the property. He went to visit the owner, but found that he was not at home. On the next day when he made an appointment with him, the owner said that about three o'clock he was awakened and could not sleep for two hours.

"While he was thus lying awake," Mr. Muller states, "his mind was all the time occupied about the piece of land . . . and he determined that if I should apply for it, he would not only let me have it, but for a hundred and twenty pounds an acre instead of two hundred, the price he had previously asked for it. How good is the Lord."

Thus Mr. Muller secured the land for $2,800 less than he would have the night before.

After the land was bought, he continued his daily season of intercourse with God for funds. Step by step he waited upon the Lord to supply all that was needed in the construction of so large a building.

Gifts varying in size from a farthing to five and six hundred pounds made Mr. Muller's heart glad. On January 25, 1847, he entered in his diary, "Therefore with increased earnestness I have given myself unto prayer, importuning the Lord that He would . . . speedily send the remainder of the amount . . . and I have increasingly of late felt that the time is drawing near." This was fourteen months and three weeks after he first began asking God for a new building, and it was to be a grand day in the work of God. Let his words tell the story.

"I arose from my knees this morning full of confidence. . . . About an hour, after I had prayed thus, there was given me the sum of two thousand pounds for the Building Fund. Thus I have received altogether £9,285 3s. 9½d. Four hundred and forty-seven days I have had day by day to wait upon God before the sum reached the above amount."

When this princely gift came he was neither excited nor surprised, he "could only sit before God, and admire Him, like David in II Samuel, chapter 7." Finally he threw himself flat on his face and burst forth in thanksgivings to God and "in surrendering my heart afresh to Him for His blessed service."

Then came other gifts, among them two thousand pounds, followed by another of one thousand, and on July 5, 1847, when eleven thousand and sixty-two pounds had been donated, the building was finally begun.

This was after the help of the Lord had been daily sought for six hundred and seven days. As the building progressed funds increased until fifteen thousand, seven hundred and eighty-four pounds were received. The last donation was for two thousand pounds from a man who brought the money in notes so that his bankers might not know of his liberality.

After the building was finished, all expenses met, trustees organized, there was a balance of £776, which afforded "a manifest proof that the Lord can not only supply us with all we need in His service simply in answer to prayer, but that He can also give us even more than we need."

All of these gifts, it must be remembered, were

wrestled from the hand of God through Mr. Muller's prayers. He prayed definitely and diligently. God answered just as specifically. In addition to praying in the building funds, Mr. Muller also bore the burden of caring for the houses on Wilson Street and their one hundred and thirty children. Never once did he despair of the Lord's willingness and ability to give. He knew he was centered in God's will, and asking and receiving were natural complements.

On July 21 he records asking God for four specific things: his own personal needs, for the building fund, for the orphanage on Wilson Street and for the Institution. A gentleman from Devonshire called upon him and made a donation of twenty pounds, specifying that it was for the four identical things about which he had been talking to God. "Thus I received, *at the very moment that I had been asking God,* four answers to my prayers."

On June 18, 1849, more than twelve years after beginning the work, the orphans were transferred from the rented houses on Wilson Street to the new house on Ashley Down. Throughout the year other children arrived until by May 26 of the following year there were 275 children in the house, the whole number of those connected with the institution being 308, who daily depended upon the prayers of Mr. Muller for their sustenance.

On Saturday, June 23, after moving to Ashley Down, God marvelously began supplying the needs. A man while walking through the home with Mr. Muller exclaimed, "These children must consume a great deal of provisions," and while speaking he drew from his pocket-book notes to the amount of a hundred. On the same day came six casks of treacle and six loaves of sugar. Information arrived that a friend had just then purchased a thousand pounds of rice for the children.

"So bountifully has the Lord been pleased to help of late, that I have not only been able to meet all the extraordinary heavy expenses connected with moving . . . filling the stores . . . but I have more than five hundred pounds in hand to begin house-keeping in the new Orphan House. . . . After all the many and long-continued seasons of great trial of faith for thirteen years and two months, during which the orphans were in Wilson Street, the Lord dismisses us from thence in comparative abundance. His name be praised."

So gracious had the Lord dealt with Mr. Muller that no sooner had he housed his children in their new home and filled it to capacity than his faith began reaching forth for larger quarters, so that he might care for a thousand children. This was in spite of the fact that each day had to be supplied through constant and long seasons of prayers. No great abundance of money was coming in to meet these daily needs.

On December 5, 1850, he wrote, "It is now sixteen years and nine months this evening since I began the Scriptural Knowledge Institution for Home and Abroad. . . . It is so large that I have not only disbursed since its commencement about fifty thousand pounds sterling, but that also the current expenses . . . amount to above six thousand pounds a year. *I did 'open my mouth wide' this evening fifteen years ago, and the Lord has filled it.* The new Orphan House is filled by three hundred orphans. . . . My labor is abundant."

Mr. Muller's heart was literally consumed with passion for God and orphans. Just before Christmas of

1850, he declared, "I have served Satan much in my younger years, and I desire now with all my might to serve God during the remaining days of my earthly pilgrimage. I am forty-five years and three months old. Every day decreases the number of days that I have to stay on earth. I therefore desire with all my might to work. There are vast multitudes of orphans to be provided for."

God burned upon his soul the idea of another and larger house each day, and he affirmed, "By the help of God I shall continue day by day to wait upon Him in prayer concerning this thing till He shall bid me act."

On January 14, 1851, he went over the old grounds once again for and against a new house to care for seven hundred more children, and as previously, faith prevailed, and he declared that God would enable him to carry it through.

A couple weeks later he affirmed that he did not doubt that God would be honored by his asking largely for this purpose; since it was his duty to enlarge his quarters. Accordingly he set the sum of £35,000 as the goal to be sought before beginning the work. In May of that year he let his intentions be known. Realizing that the amount was large, his heart leaped with secret joy, "for the greater the difficulty to be overcome, the more it would be seen to the glory of God how much can be done by prayer and faith."

At once gifts began to come in, the first being the sum of sixpence, the donation of an orphan. While reading Hebrews 6:15, "And so after he had patiently endured, he obtained the promise," his heart was immediately uplifted. He had become somewhat discouraged with the slowness and the smallness of the gifts as they arrived.

The year 1851 was a test of his faith, but the following came as a triumph of his trust. In March of that year he was encouraged by a gift of £999, and when the accounts for the twelve months were closed the fund stood at £3,530, which included the seven hundred and seventy-six pounds left from the first building fund.

At this time 360 orphans were awaiting admission, and as applications arrived Mr. Muller's faith increased. For where there was a need he felt God would surely supply. At the beginning of 1853 several Christians together promised approximately $40,500 to be distributed among the various funds, $30,000 of which was to go into the Building Fund.

Mr. Muller thus realized that there was no limit upon God's willingness and ability to provide large donations.

As the money increased, Mr. Muller began looking for a suitable building site, but when none was found close by the first house, he decided to construct two buildings instead of one. The first was to house 400 girls, and the other 300 boys. He had sufficient funds at hand to construct the first building, so he decided to proceed with the first house. There were at this time 715 orphans seeking admission to the home.

Donations came from practically every civilized nation on earth. Muller's "Narrative" had been translated into several languages and the story of his work had spread from country to country.

In spite of the large gifts that continued to flow in, he was a faithful servant in the smaller things. On October 12, 1852, he made this Journal entry: "By sale of rags and bones twelve shillings sixpence. I copy literally from the receipt book. We seek to make the best of everything. As a steward of public money, I feel it right that even these articles should be turned into money; nor could we expect answers to our prayers if knowingly there were any waste allowed in connection with the work."

In these times of larger vision and work, God led him day by day to trust for supplies. Speaking of two weeks during the Christmas holidays of 1852-53, he said, "We had nothing in advance of our wants. Means came in only as they were required for pressing needs. We ask no human being for help. . . . We depend alone upon God."

While the work of building the new house was in progress, Mr. Muller continued to keep his requests before the Lord. Large gifts were sent in, one for $15,000 and another for $20,000. An offer was also received to fill the 300 large windows in the house with glass.

Of this incident Mr. Muller avows, "It is worthy of note that the glass was not contracted for this time, as in the case of the House already built. This, no doubt, was under the ordering of our Heavenly Father."

About a year before the building's completion approximately $150,000 was on hand for the expense. At one time he was examining the 150 gas burners when he felt constrained to return home suddenly. On arriving he found a check for £1,000 from a person who "concluded it would be good and profitable to invest a little in the Orphan Houses."

Finally on November 12, 1857, just seven years after the idea had burned in Mr. Muller's soul, the New Orphan House, No. 2, was opened. He wrote on this day, "The long looked-for and long prayed-for day has now arrived when the desire of my heart was granted to me, to be able to open the house for four hundred additional orphans. . . . How precious this was to me . . . having day by day prayed for a blessing for seven years."

When the house was opened there were left over in the fund for the third house a balance of approximately twenty-three hundred pounds. This sum was believed to be the earnest of the entire amount needed for the third building's construction. Accordingly his faith took hold of God for another building which would house three hundred children.

He had planned to build this by the first house, but when the time arrived to begin construction this seemed unwise. So the old search for a suited site began once more. After much searching and no little vexation a plot of eleven and a half acres across the road from the present buildings was secured. The price was high, more than $16,000, but since it was so close to the other buildings it seemed wise to Mr. Muller to invest God's money in it.

Since there were so many applications for entry, it was decided to make this large enough to care for 450 children instead of the original 300, and in confirmation of this a gift shortly arrived for £7,000, to be followed afterward by another £1,700. Glass was again promised for the 309 windows, and on July, 1859, the builders began their work.

Many large donations came in, so that in May, 1861, Mr. Muller was able to announce that the sum of £46,666 had been donated for Houses No. 2 and 3, which exceeded the original amount prayed for by £11,666.

God's hand lavishly began to pour out funds to care for the children while the house was being constructed, for there was more than $45,000 to the credit of the current expense fund before House No. 3 was occupied.

On March 12, 1862, the house was opened. This brought Mr. Muller great joy. He wrote about this event, "It was in November 1850 that my mind became exercised about enlarging the orphan work from 300 to 1,000 orphans, and subsequently to 1,150. . . . From November, 1850, to this day, March 12, 1862, not one single day has been allowed to pass without this contemplated enlargement being brought before God in prayer, and generally more than once a day.

"Observe then . . . how long it may be before a full answer to our prayers, even to thousands and tens of thousands of prayers, is granted. . . . I did without the least doubt and wavering look for more than eleven years for the full answer."

Nor did God want the work to stop with the third house. After the House No. 1 was finished there was a balance of £776 in the building fund along with £500 for current expenses. When House No. 2 was completed the balance available for expenses was £2,292. When the last house was finished the balance on hand for current expenses was £10,309.

This does not include the amount of money necessary to carry on the work of the Scriptural Institution, whose expenses ran into the thousands of pounds each year. All of this was brought in through prayer alone.

"As in the case of No. 2," Mr. Muller states, "so also in the case of the New Orphan House No. 3, I had daily prayed for the needed helpers and assistants for the various departments. Before a stone was laid,

I began to pray for this, and as the building progressed, I continued day by day to bring the matter before God."

Before the third house was completed such was the pressure for larger accommodations to make room for the hundreds of applications which came in, that Mr. Muller conceived of building two more houses to accommodate an additional 850 orphans, making the total 2,000.

He felt that God would have him improve his special talent of trust and faith for daily supplies and building funds by taking this new step in his spiritual pilgrimage. Once impressed that a course was the divine will, Mr. Muller was never long in putting it into operation.

He knew but one course of procedure . . . to trust daily for supplies and believe daily for building funds. And this hand to mouth existence—*from God's hand to Muller's and the orphans' mouths* — had been so gracious for the long years past that Mr. Muller did not hesitate to step forth again on a venture that would within a short span of years provide a home for almost twice as many children as he then housed.

Chapter VIII

UNDERTAKING GREATER THINGS FOR GOD

Mr. Muller desired to witness further for Christ. When he had housed 1150 orphans, he wanted the world to know that God was able to supply the necessary funds to care for 2,000. This became his prayer goal, and no sooner had the children moved into House No. 3 than he dreamed of two more plants—dreams gradually to come to pass.

For four years between moving into the more recently constructed houses and the commencement of House No. 4, Mr. Muller prayed constantly that God would supply the money for the new building. During those times it was necessary to beseech God for daily food. But the God of Elijah was also the God of Muller, Who heard His child cry for sustenance.

In little matters as well as large he took his petitions to the Lord. When workers were hard to find, or proved unsuitable, Mr. Muller asked God to furnish the right ones. We find him saying, "Instead of praying once a day about this matter, as we had been doing day by day for years, we met daily three times, to bring this before God."

There was no detail too insignificant to take to the Lord in prayer. He lived literally according to the passage, "In all things by prayer and supplication, with thanksgiving, let your requests be made known unto God." He looked to the heavenly Father for food, shelter, for suited teachers and assistants, which were matters of great import. But when details called for attention, they were also subjects of prayer. For example, it became hard to find suited places for the older boys to work during the summer of 1862, so Muller carried this petition to the Father's throne.

"We had several boys ready to be apprenticed; but there were no applications made by masters for apprentices. . . . If all other difficulties were out of the way, the master must also be willing to receive the apprentice into his own family. Under these circumstances, we again gave ourselves to prayer, as we had done for more than twenty years before, concerning this thing. . . . We remembered how good the Lord has been to us in having helped us hundreds of times before in this matter. . . . The difficulty was entirely overcome by prayer, as every one of the boys, whom it was desirable to send out, has been sent out."

In spite of the daily care for the homes, with their various problems, Mr. Muller never let up in his prayers that God would make it possible for the work to be enlarged. Each week new applications for entrance were coming in. He could not easily say, "There is no more room," when he remembered that during the many years since he first rented the House on Wilson Street, God had enabled him to build larger quarters as the need arose.

The longed-for enlargement of the work would cost at least £50,000, and would increase the current expense fund from $100,000 to $175,000 a year. "But my hope," Mr. Muller said, "is in God, and in Him alone. I am not a fanatic or enthusiast, but, as all who

know me are well aware, a calm, cool, quiet, calcu-
lating business man; and therefore I should be utterly
overwhelmed, looking at it naturally. But as the whole
of this work was commenced, and ever has been gone
on with, in faith . . . so it is also regarding this enlargement. I look to the Lord alone for helpers, land,
means and everything else needed. I have pondered
the difficulties for months and have looked steadily
at every one of them; but *faith in God has put them
aside.*"

Children cried for admission and Muller believed
that "the Father of the fatherless" would not turn
a deaf ear to his prayer to shelter them. He was again
moved with the idea of proving more fully to the world
that *"the living God is still, as found a thousand years
ago, the Living God."*

Hundreds of thousands of people throughout the
world had heard of his work, and many of them had
their faith strengthened to undertake greater things in
the name of the Living God, because Mr. Muller had
shown them that God was able. He desired supremely
that God might be honored and souls brought into the
kingdom. When his faith became certain that the new
step was willed of God, he decided to go forward
at once.

"Many and great may be the difficulties," says Mr.
Muller. "Thousands and tens of thousands of prayers
may have to ascend to God before the full answer is
obtained; much exercise of faith and patience may
be required; but in the end it will again be seen that
His servant, who trusted in Him, has not been con-
founded."

The first donations for House No. 5 arrived before
they had moved into House No. 4, and consisted of

5 rupees, 6 annas, 3 senams, 3 Spanish coins, and 3 other silver coins. This was on June 6, 1861, and a month later he found a check for £2,000 at his house from a friend, who was "thankful to God for the privilege of being a fellow-helper in the work of caring for the orphans."

In the following January two other large donations of approximately $20,000 arrived, which, as with even the smallest gift, Mr. Muller received as coming in answer to his prayers. "Every donation," he observes, "brings me nearer the contemplated enlargement."

Slowly did the gifts come in during the first year or so, but his faith was unwavering in the fact that God, in His own good time, would supply all the necessary funds. "I continue in believing prayer," he states at a time when gifts had been small. "I have not been allowed to have a shadow of doubt as to whether God can and will give me the means; but day by day, in the full assurance of faith, I renew my requests before God; and generally day by day the amount of the building fund is . . . increased. I then give thanks and ask for more."

On October 3, when a seasonal gift of £5,000 arrived from a friend who did not wish his name to be made known, the fund amounted to £27,000, and Mr. Muller's faith led him to look for a suited plot of ground for the new building enterprise.

Across the road from the present buildings were 18 acres of land, for which he had been praying. "My eyes," he states, "had been for years directed to a beautiful piece of land. . . . Hundreds of times had I prayed, within recent years, that God would count me worthy to be allowed to erect on this ground two more Orphan Houses. . . . I might have bought it years ago, but that would have been going before the Lord. I had money enough in hand to have paid for it, but I desired patiently, submissively, to wait God's own time, and for Him to mark it clearly and distinctly that His time was come."

The price was staggeringly high throughout the years, but when God was ready for Mr. Muller to take this new leap of faith the owner sold the land for $7,500 less than he originally asked.

In March, 1866, with a building fund of £34,002, 2s. on hand, Mr. Muller found that construction prices had risen, and it would take approximately £7,000 more to finish the work than he had estimated. This handicap he found to be of the Lord, for on deeper study and prayer, he decided it would be better to build two houses than one. So he let the contract for House No. 4.

Concerning this change in plans he wrote, "I will not sign contracts, which I had not money in hand to meet. Should it be said . . . 'God has not money enough to pay for His own work' . . . If it shall please the Lord, by January 1, 1867, to give me about £7,000 more than I now have on hand, the contract for No. 5 will be signed."

It is gratifying to know that God supplied the money by the above stated time, and the contract was duly let. This was an hour of thanksgiving to God, for "thousands of times," he affirms, "I have asked the Lord for the means for building these two houses, and now I have to the full received the answer."

The contract price for the two buildings was £41,147, or $205,735, which Mr. Muller had prayed in, plus an additional $100,000 to care for the current expenses yearly during the five years since the first gift for the new buildings arrived. This made a total of approximately three-quarters of a million dollars in five years which this man's prayers brought into the coffers of God's kingdom for the sole purpose of caring for orphans.

As on previous occasions the window glass was donated for the new houses. It required ten thousand pounds to furnish the buildings, which also came as the result of Muller's prayers. In February, 1868, he announced that all necessary funds were in hand. After waiting on God daily, and often several times a day, for nearly seven years the end of his prayer came at last, and Mr. Muller gave himself to thanksgiving and praise to the Lord for once again "filling his mouth" after he had opened it wider than ever before. The total sum required for the two buildings reached the staggering amount of fifty-eight thousand pounds.

House No. 4 was opened on November 5, 1868, and two years later on January 6, 1870, the long-prayed for day arrived when the last house, No. 5, was thrown open to occupancy.

It required an immense amount of labor to transfer children from one house to another, to fill in vacancies, and to select from the hundreds of applications the children whom Mr. Muller decided to be the most suited and the most in need to fill the houses to overflowing.

Mr. Muller declared, "In the mighty monument of prayer raised there was afforded not merely a Christian home for 2,050 destitute orphan children—great indeed as that was—but a supreme and striking object-lesson in simple, child-like faith, a signal evidence of Christ's power and love, sufficient to make men pause, and wonder, and enquire, and—God grant it more and more—believe."

"Thus have been gathered," writes A. T. Pierson, "the facts about the erection of this great monument to a prayer-hearing God on Ashley Down, though the work of building covered so many years. Between the first decision to build, in 1845, and the opening of the third house, in 1862, nearly seventeen years had elapsed, and before No. 5 was opened, in 1870, twenty-five. The work was one in its plan and purpose. At each new stage it supplies only a wider application and illustration of the same laws of life and conduct, as, from the outset of the work in Bristol, had with growing power controlled George Muller.

"His supreme aim was the glory of God; his sole resort, believing prayer; his one trusted oracle, the inspired Word; his one divine Teacher, the Holy Spirit. One step taken in faith and prayer had prepared for another; one act of trust had made him bolder to venture upon another, implying a greater apparent risk and therefore demanding more implicit trust."

Answered prayer was rewarded faith. New risks undertaken only proved there was no risk at all in confidently leaning upon the strong arm of the Almighty.

The buildings impressed one with their spaciousness, seventeen hundred windows in all, and accommodations for more than two thousand people. They were substantial, made of stone and built for permanency. While scrupulously plain, they were still excellent examples of construction whose end is utility rather than beauty. In building them Muller's rule was economy. This went to the smallest items, even the furniture being unpretentious. There is little or no embellishment.

Mr. Muller subordinated everything to the one purpose of demonstrating the fact that God still hears prayer. He felt that he was a public steward of God's property and he hesitated to spend even a penny needlessly. He made the buildings plain for he felt that the orphans would be put into service in similar surroundings. He studied to promote health and education and to school the orphans to be content with the necessities, and not the luxuries, of life.

Cleanness, neatness and method everywhere was in evidence about the buildings and the grounds. The tracts of land, adjoining the buildings, were set apart as gardens, where the boys found their work and exercise. Throughout the houses care was exhibited in arrangement. Each child had a square and numbered compartment for clothes. The boys had each three suits and the girls five dresses.

Mr. Muller, with so large a family to oversee, laid out the daily life with regularity, and demanded that everything be conducted with the punctuality of a clock. The children got up at six and at seven were ready for their pre-breakfast duties. Breakfast was at eight, followed with a half-hour for service before school opened at ten. Dinner at one led up to an afternoon of school work, followed by an hour and a half of outdoor exercise, and then the six o'clock meal. Mr. Muller asked God for simple food, yet nutritious, such as bread, oatmeal, milk, soups, rice, meat and vegetables.

When the Orphan Houses were finally filled, Mr. Muller sought one end. "We aim at this," he observes, "that if any of them do not turn out well, temporally or spiritually, and do not become useful members of society, it shall not at least be our fault."

There was a steady increase in expenses demanded by the larger family of orphans cared for, but Mr. Muller's faith was sufficiently strong in the Lord to keep the supplies on hand.

On May 26, 1861, he writes, "At the close of the period I find that the total expenditure for all the various objects was £24,700 16s. 4d., or £67 13s. 5¾d. per day, all the year around. During the coming year I expect the expenses to be considerably greater. But God, Who has helped me these many years, will, I believe, help me in the future also. You see, esteemed reader, how the Lord, in His faithful love helped us year after year . . . *He never failed us.*"

Under date of October 21, 1868, he enters in his diary, "As the days come, we make known our requests to Him, for our outgoings have now been for several years at the rate of more than one hundred pounds each day; but though the expenses have been so great, *He has never failed us.*"

Year by year this increase of needs followed by God's graciously supplying them is noted in his Journal. Writing on July 28, 1874, he says, "It had for months appeared to me, as if the Lord meant . . . to bring us back to the state of things in which we were for more than ten years, from August 1838, until April, 1849, when we had day by day, almost without interruption, to look to Him for our daily supplies, and for a great part of the time, from meal to meal. The difficulties appeared to me indeed very great, as the Institution is now twenty times larger than it was then, and our purchases are to be made in a wholesale way; but I am comforted by the knowledge that God is aware of all this . . .

"The funds were thus expended; but God, our infinitely rich Treasurer, remains to us. It is this which gives me peace. Moreover, if it pleases him, with a work requiring about £44,000 a year, to make me do again at the evening of my life, what I did from August, 1838, to April, 1849, I am not only prepared for it, but gladly again I would pass through all these trials of faith . . . if He only might be glorified and His church and the world be benefited.

"Often and often this last point has of late passed through my mind and I have placed myself in the position of having no means at all left, and two thousand and one hundred persons not only daily at the table, but with everything else to be provided for, and all funds gone; 189 missionaries to be assisted, and nothing whatever left; about one hundred schools, with about nine thousand scholars in them, to be entirely supported, and no means for them in hand; about four millions of tracts and tens of thousands of copies of the Holy Scriptures yearly now to be sent out, and all the money expended.

"Invariably, however, . . . I have said to myself: 'God Who raised up this work through me, God Who has led me generally year after year to enlarge it, God Who has supported this work now for more than forty years, will still help . . . and He will provide me with what I need in the future also . . !'"

On the following day, to show how God honored Muller's trust, he received £217 up until early afternoon. "We thanked God for it," he says, triumphant in his faith, "and *asked for more*. When the meeting for prayer was over, there was handed me a letter from Scotland, containing £73 17s. 10d., and a paper with 13s. This was the *immediate* answer to prayer for more means."

On August 12 of that year he states his income for the week to have been more than £897. On September 16, he writes, "Just after having again prayed for the payment of legacies . . . I had a legacy receipt sent for the payment of a legacy of £1,800." A week later he enters this item in his Journal. "Income today £5,365 13s. 6d.," all of which except approximately £32 came in one donation—"The Lord be praised."

During those faith-trying times Mr. Muller had a faithful wife who bore his burdens with him. Side by side they prayed for many years, faith together taking hold of God's promises. But Mrs. Muller was not permitted to remain by her husband's side till the end. She lived just a month after opening the Fifth Orphan House. Concerning this Mr. Muller writes:

"Feb. 6, 1870. On Oct. 7, 1830 (therefore 39 years and four months since) the Lord gave me my most valuable, lovely and holy wife. Her value to me and the blessing God made her to be to me is beyond description. This blessing was continued to me till this day, when, in the afternoon, about four o'clock, the Lord took her to himself."

The funeral was on February 11, when many thousands of persons were in attendance. About 1,200 of the orphans who were able to walk followed the procession and hundreds of beloved fellow Christians walked with the group. "I myself," he says, "sustained by the Lord to the utmost, performed the service in the chapel, in the cemetery, etc. Shortly after the funeral I was very unwell, but as soon as I was sufficiently recovered I preached my late dear wife's funeral sermon."

In this sermon, preached from the text, "Thou art good, and doest good" (Psa. 119:68), he drew a picture of a sweet and simple life, made dearer through holy service. He described his wife as "the mother of the orphans."

"Every day," he said in the funeral sermon, "I miss her more and more. Every day I see more and more how great is her loss to the orphans. Yet, without an effort, my inmost soul habitually joys in the joy of the loved departed one. . . . God alone has done it; we are satisfied with Him."

In three divisions he dealt with the text: "The Lord was good and did good: first, in giving her to me; second, in so long leaving her with me; and third, in taking her from me."

Sixteen months after Mrs. Muller's death, on November 16, 1871, Mr. James Wright married Mr. Muller's daughter, and was designated as his successor in case of the founder's death. When Mr. Wright accepted this responsibility, Mr. Muller wrote:

"By the Lord's kindness I am able to work as heretofore . . . yet, as I am sixty-six years of age, I cannot conceal from myself that it is of great importance for the work that I should obtain a measure of relief. . . . On this account, I have therefore not only appointed Mr. Wright as my successor, in the event of my death, but have also associated him at present with me in the direction of the Institution.

This man of faith through storm and stress still rejoiced in the Lord, for when he closed the year of his wife's death, he affirms, "Though the current expenses of the Institution were far greater during the past year than during any of the previous thirty-five years, yet we abounded more than ever."

Mr. Muller grew restless in contemplation of his daughter's marriage, and felt his lonely condition keenly. He realized the need of someone to share his toils and prayers, and help in the Lord's work. The persuasion grew upon him that he should remarry. After much prayer he determined to ask Miss Susannah Grace Sangar to become his wife, having known her for more than twenty-five years, and believing her to be well fitted to be his helper in the Lord.

They were married fourteen days after his daughter's marriage to Mr. Wright. The second wife was of one mind concerning the stewardship of the Lord's property. They were to live together for more than twenty-three years, and when God took his second wife home, Mr. Muller again preached the funeral sermon. For eight years after the death of his first wife Mr. Muller could not understand God's purpose in her death, but time showed him that "All things work together for good to them that love the Lord."

For Mr. Muller was about to commence the most strenuous years of his career. God wanted the story of faith to be carried to other lands, and in the person of Mr. Wright he furnished a man upon whose shoulders should rest the responsibility of caring for the home, while Mr. Muller traveled throughout the world with his message of trust.

"All at once, while in the midst of these fatiguing journeys and exposures to varying climates, it flashed upon Mr. Muller that his first wife, who had died in her seventy-third year, *could never have undertaken these tours*, and that the Lord had thus, in taking her, left him free to make these extensive journeys. She would have been over fourscore years old when these tours began . . . whereas, the second Mrs. Muller, who, at that time, was not yet fifty-seven, was both by her age and strength fully equal to the strain thus put upon her," writes A. T. Pierson, who was personally acquainted with the second Mrs. Muller.

CHAPTER IX

CARRYING FAITH'S MESSAGE TO THE WORLD

MR. MULLER'S heart always rang true to the missionary vision. Five times within the first eight years of his conversion he offered himself as a missionary. Each time God blocked the way. Now at the evening of his life God was to send him forth a missionary in a broader sense, with an appeal that would reach many millions of people.

God had seasoned him in the school of prayer for decades. In his seventieth year he was to go forth to the nations with a message of trust and faith. For seventeen years, most of his time and energy were to be engaged in this new type of work. He had already been a missionary through the Institution which assisted many Christian workers in foreign fields and distributed thousands of Bibles and millions of tracts.

In 1874 Mrs. Muller's health compelled him to seek a change of climate, and he took her to the Isle of Wight, where he preached for a friend, himself an experienced minister. The preacher said to Mr. Muller, "This is the happiest day of my life."

Thinking upon this remark, how his message had stirred the preacher, Mr. Muller decided that no longer, as for the past forty-three years, would he confine his ministry to Bristol, but felt that God would have him

91

go from city to city, country to country, to benefit both the Church and the world by his experience of trust and life of faith.

After many days in prayer, he laid down seven motives which led him to undertake this world-wide mission. These were: to preach the gospel in its simplicity; to lead believers to know their converted state and realize their privileges in God; to bring believers back to the Bible; to promote among Christians a spirit of brotherly love; to strengthen, through example of how God had answered his prayers, true Christians in their life of trust; to promote separateness from the world, as was displayed in his founding the Institution; and to fix in the minds of Christians the hope of Christ's coming.

On March 26,1875, he began a series of seventeen missionary tours that would take him to forty-two nations, covering two hundred thousand miles by land and water. He preached many thousands of times, and from his own estimate during these tours, he spoke to three million people. "The whole of the heavy expenses of these tours was supplied, as in the case of all his other wants, simply and solely in answer to believing prayers," writes Fred Warne, Mr. Muller's first biographer.

He had previously made two tours to Germany in the interest of Christian work while the orphanage was small, but his important life career of missions had its commencement on March 26, in his seventieth year. It was not a long trip, though he terms it "the beginning of my missionary tours."

He went from Bristol to Brighton, and Sunderland. While on his way to Sunderland he spoke at the Metropolitan Tabernacle, where Charles Spurgeon was pastor.

He preached at other leading places such as the Mildmay Park Conference and the Edinburgh Castle. The tour closed after ten weeks on June 5, during which time he delivered seventy addresses.

The second of his tours, in conjunction with his wife, commenced less than six weeks later, on August 14, in which case he felt a desire to follow up the revival work of Moody and Sankey. Mr. Muller felt that the evangelists' short visits to the various cities did not give the converts time to be led to the higher attainments of grace, and he wanted to build his messages toward this end.

Accordingly he addressed many large audiences in London, Glasgow, Dublin and Liverpool, and in other smaller places. In some cities, especially at Dundee, Glasgow, Liverpool and Dublin, his audiences numbered from two to six thousand. The tour lasted nearly eleven months, and when it closed in July of 1876, he had preached three hundred and six times, an average of one sermon a day. So great was the success of these meetings that he received a hundred invitations which he could not accept.

When asked about the results of these missionary labors, he replied, "The day of the Lord alone will reveal it. Here on earth, but little can be known, comparatively, of the fruit of our labors; yet, as far as I have been permitted to see, even here, there is good reason to believe that I have not been directed to one single place regarding which there was not manifest proof that the Lord sent me there."

The third tour took him to the Continent, and commenced in August, 1876, and closed in June of the following year. This embraced Paris, various places in Switzerland, Prussia, Holland, Alsace, Wurtemburg, etc. Everywhere his preaching created a considerable stir among the Christian people.

At Stuttgart, Mr. Muller held an interview with the Queen of Wurtemburg, who at the Palace asked him many questions about the Orphanage in Bristol. At Darmstadt by request he spoke in the drawing-room of the Court Preacher, at which the mother of Prince Louis of Hesse, and other princes and princesses were present. While in Berlin the cousin of Prince Bismarck traveled 125 miles to hear him, whose "Narrative" had been a blessing to his spiritual life.

While at Halle he delivered two messages in Franke's Orphan Institution, which had been the seed idea leading Mr. Muller to found his Bristol Houses. Near Nimenguen, Holland, he also visited an orphanage for 450 children, which had been established by an evangelist in total dependence upon God, as the result of reading about Muller's success at the Ashley Down orphanage.

"Similarly," Mr. Muller observes, "very many Orphan Institutions have been begun in various parts of the world, the founders being encouraged through what God has done for us in Bristol. His Name be magnified."

When this Continental tour closed there were sixty written invitations which he could not accept. Through his writings Mr. Muller had become as well known on the Continent as in England.

His fourth tour led him to the United States and Canada, for he had been receiving many invitations to speak in these nations during the past months. Hence he took it as God's will that he should carry his faith messages across the ocean. From August, 1877, to July of the following year he traveled throughout the New World.

Landing at Quebec, where he spoke, he swept down the Atlantic seaboard, speaking in the principal cities. Then he crossed the nation to the Pacific Coast, and returned by way of Salt Lake City—the stronghold of Mormonism—and back again to New York City. For ten months he covered this vast area with his spiritual life messages, and crowded the largest auditoriums to capacity.

He spoke to congregations of Germans, and in the South to many colored people. Many preachers' meetings were conducted where his message was directed to the ministers of the people. These activities afforded him greater pleasure than any others. Theological seminary and university meetings were also greatly beloved by this apostle of faith. He realized that he was sowing the seeds of his doctrine of trust in fertile minds that would later spread the truth to their growing congregations. Various denominations opened their doors to him to speak to their ministers, Sunday school conventions and similar groups.

Dr. Talmage's Tabernacle in Brooklyn held a warm spot in his heart, for here he was welcomed and spoke to many leading people of the nation. By appointment at the White House, he was received by President and Mrs. Hayes, who inquired about the success of his orphanage work.

In many places Mr. Muller met orphans who had once been at his home in Bristol. Often he would meet, as he did coming out of Yosemite, someone who would rush up and ask to shake hands with him, saying, "I have read your 'Life of Trust,' and it has been a blessing to my soul."

The tour ended in July, 1878, during which he had spoken three hundred and eight times and traveled 19,274 miles.

"It is important that I state," Mr. Muller remarked on returning to Bristol, "that my preaching tour in the United States was not set about for the purpose of collecting money for the Institution . . . but only that by my experience and knowledge of Divine things, I might benefit Christians . . . and that I might preach the Gospel to those who knew not the Lord. . . . The donations handed me for the Institution would not meet one half of its average expenses for one single day."

Before undertaking his fifth missionary journey, he stayed eight weeks at Bristol, overseeing the work of the orphanage and giving his wife an opportunity to rest. On September 5, 1878, they started off for a second visit to the Continent, where he preached in English, German and French. In Spain and Italy, which languages he could not use, he spoke through an interpreter. Many doors were opened to him among the poor, but in some places, such as in the Riviera, he had access to the aristocracy and nobility who had gathered there for their health.

At Barcelona, Spain, he visited ten of the day schools which were entirely supported by the Scriptural Knowledge Institution, and at Madrid he spoke to five schools dependent upon the same agency. In Rome he had the pleasure of speaking and at Naples he visited Vesuvius. On looking down into the crater he exclaimed, "What cannot God do." He visited the Vaudois valleys, where so many martyrs had laid down their lives for Christ's sake, and he was deeply moved to accomplish more for his Master than before.

When he arrived in Bristol on June 18, 1879, he

had been absent nine months and twelve days, and had preached 286 times in 46 towns and cities of several nations.

Ten weeks after completing his last journey, the call of America became strong upon his spirit, and he and Mrs. Muller set sail on the last week of August for the United States and Canada. This was his sixth journey, and lasted until June, 1880, when he felt constrained to return to Bristol, where he wanted to relieve Mr. Wright and his daughter of the orphanage responsibility for a while. He had visited 42 different places and had spoken 299 times. He found there were 154 written invitations which he had not been able to accept.

Praying over these invitations led Mr. Muller to decide he should make his seventh journey to take in the United States once more, that he might keep the embers of faith stirred up in this country. So on September 15, 1880, he and his wife returned to the States by way of Canada, and remained until the close of May of the following year. Three months of this time were spent in New York, where he conducted 93 meetings, 38 of which were in German. During this visit he spoke 250 times in all.

Considering the weather that winter, for a man seventy-five years old his labors were prodigious. "That winter," Mrs. Muller writes, "was the coldest that has been known in New York for thirty years, and the many long drives my beloved husband took at night . . . when the weather was most severe, were very trying. . . . Constrained by the love of Christ, however, he persevered in a service that would have been considered, by most persons of his age, an arduous undertaking."

On returning to British soil again, he relieved Mr. Wright, upon whose shoulders the heavy burdens of the home rested, for a period of eight weeks, when a strong desire motivated him to visit the missionaries in the East. On August 23, 1881, he set out for the Continent, where he spoke in Switzerland and Germany, hoping to revive the low state of grace which existed in these countries.

The visit was extended to Alexandria, Cairo and Port Said, whence he traveled to the Holy Land. His soul revelled in the sacred scenes where the Master had lived. He visited through Palestine the many places of religious interest, such as Gethsemane and Golgotha, the Mount of Olives and Bethany, Bethlehem and Jerusalem. He went into Turkey and Greece, speaking at such places as Constantinople, Athens, Rome and Florence. He preached in English and German on this tour, and through an interpreter in Arabic, Armenian, Turkish and modern Greek.

After a very brief rest he undertook his ninth tour on August 8, 1882, which extended until June 1, 1883. He traveled in Germany, Austria, Hungary, Bohemia, Russia and Poland. It was his special privilege to speak at Kroppenstadt, his birthplace, after an absence of sixty-four years. Here he was asked to give his life story. The largest building was crowded to overflowing.

In Russia he spoke at St. Petersburg (now Leningrad), and was the guest of Princess Lieven. At Lodz, Poland, a letter of invitation, signed by most all of the population, asked him to remain with them longer.

Returning to Bristol, a new desire burned within him to see the Orient, and to visit the scenes amid which he had dreamed of working when a young minister.

On September 26, 1883, his tenth tour began when he set his face toward the Orient. Nearly sixty years earlier he had planned to be a missionary to the East Indies, and now the Lord was permitting him to carry out this ambition in a new and strange way, for India was to be the twenty-third country visited in his tours.

He traveled more than 21,000 miles, and spoke two hundred times to missionaries, Christian workers, European residents, and the natives. He was greatly elated at seeing the orphanage at Colar. He felt that in this his seventy-ninth year, God had abundantly blessed him, for there was great evidence that this tour was used of the Lord to quicken the spiritual life of the missionaries, and to awaken the native workers to their need of a life of full dependence upon God.

On arriving in England he assumed the duties of the orphanage, but his active soul would not be content to remain long away from his evangelistic and missionary tours. During this period of his life, his consuming passion was to spread through his own preaching ministry the life of trust, as during the earlier years it had been to prove that *the living God is living still* and is able to feed orphans through one man's faith in His power.

Consequently his eleventh tour began in August and extended to October of 1884, and mainly consisted of a journey to South Wales. The twelfth tour was likewise a short one in the home country, made so through a serious indisposition. This illness, however, was short-lived and soon overcome by a rest in the Isle of Wight, which years earlier had been the inspiration of his journeyings throughout the world in interest of "the life of trust."

His thirteenth preaching mission lasted only a month

and was spent visiting the Lake District, Dundee and Liverpool, where the messages on faith quickened the consciences of many Christians to undertake more earnestly a life of trust.

In November of the same year (1885) when Mr. Muller was eighty he undertook another long foreign missionary voyage to Australia, China, Japan and the Straits of Malacca. He also included the United States in this itinerary. He desired especially to establish and encourage the missionaries in China in their arduous work. In Japan he was able to hold large mass meetings. At one meeting 2,500 Japanese heard him speak through an interpreter.

After an absence of eighteen months, he reached Bristol in June, 1887, during which time he had traveled 37,280 miles and preached wherever opportunity afforded.

There seemed to be no limit to his strength on these missionary journeys. God had poured out upon him *abundant-life* energy which enabled him to go forth and tell the world that this blessing could be theirs also.

Less than two months later, on August 12, 1887, when Muller was eighty-two years old, he set forth again on travels that would take him to South Australia, Tasmania, New Zealand, Ceylon and India. This was a twelve months' tour, used greatly of the Lord to strengthen the faith of believers wherever he spoke.

"Believers were edified," he writes, "the unconverted persons brought through my ministry to a knowledge of the Lord." He preached to large audiences of natives who listened intently to his words. The severe hot weather of Ceylon and India proved a trying experience, and he was repeatedly told that he was working too hard for a man of his age. At Calcutta the heat was so intense that upon medical advice he left, and on the way to Darjeeling he thought he was going to die. But a short rest proved a respite and soon he was able to undertake his journey once more.

While at Jubbulpore Mr. Wright cabled that his daughter, Mrs. Wright, had died. For thirty years of the fifty-eight of her life, she had worked gratuitously in the Orphan Houses. This news of her death caused Mr. Muller to cut short the tour in the East and to hasten to Bristol to relieve and comfort Mr. Wright in the time of added personal burdens and responsibilities at the Houses.

"My heart," Mr. Muller says, "remained in perfect peace because I took this affliction, as I had taken former heavy trials, out of the hand of my heavenly Father, fully realizing that He had taken her to Himself and had done therefore the very best thing that could happen, and that to me this event would work for my good."

After four months at Ashley Down he was led to go to the Continent for Mrs. Muller's health. This unintentionally developed into his sixteenth missionary tour. He spoke to crowded assemblies wherever he appeared.

"My heart has been greatly refreshed at seeing almost everywhere in Germany and Switzerland such a desire to hear the truth, notwithstanding the departure of so many persons from it."

Again he was led to return home, where he remained for a short while before the old burden for the Continent returned, and though advanced in years, now eighty-six, he set forth for Europe once more, preaching in Germany, Holland, Austria and Italy. When this twelve months' journey ended in May, 1892, it was the last extended tour the veteran missionary of the Cross was to take.

Only an unusual spiritual and physical enduement enabled a man of seventy years of age to spend seventeen years of his life traveling hundreds of thousands of miles, and preaching between six and eight thousand times outside of his home city of Bristol to more than 3,000,000 people.

Even to the end he spoke with vigor. Mr. Pierson tells of one of his sermons in Berlin when Mr. Muller was eighty-six. He urged believers never to yield to discouragement, pointing out that it was their spiritual duty to seek the deep secret of rest for their souls. "Saved believers," he declared, "can know their position in the Lord. You must become acquainted with the Scriptures the hope of your salvation." He affirmed that God alone is the satisfying portion of the soul.

In these mission tours every need was miraculously supplied. The heavy outlay for steamer and train fares, as well as hotel accommodations, was always on hand as the Lord sent it.

Often it was asked why he did not stay at home and supervise the work of the Ashley Down Houses. In his answer he said that under Mr. Wright's care the needs of the Houses were met, and to suppose that it was necessary for him to be at home in order that sufficient means should be supplied was a contradiction to the very principle upon which the work was started.

"Real trust in God is above circumstances and appearances," he affirmed.

Mr. Muller was fully convinced of the rightness of his views on this point during the third year of his missionary journeys. For in that year the income for the Scriptural Knowledge Institution was larger than it had ever been during the previous forty-four years of its existence.

He looked upon these last seventeen years as the richest and ripest he had engaged in. "Very godly and advanced Christians have told me," he remarked on this subject, "that they consider my present labors the most important of my whole life."

CHAPTER X

THE SCRIPTURAL KNOWLEDGE INSTITUTION

THE NAME of George Muller has predominately been
connected with orphanage work. This phase of his
life's investment has so greatly overshadowed his other
fields of Christian endeavor that they are often forgotten. His seventeen missionary tours were made
famous because he was looked upon as the world's
leading friend of orphans, and while he spoke of faith
and trust, his illustrations were mainly drawn from
many years of daily experience in feeding thousands
of children through prayer alone.

There was, however, another phase of his life's work
which depended solely upon his prayers as much as
the caring for his orphan houses at Ashley Down. This
was his promulgation of the Scriptural Knowledge Institution. When he was led to found the Institution
on February 20, 1834, he entered in his Journal, *"I
trust this matter is of God."*

Surely God's blessings were upon this element of
the stewardship of Mr. Muller's personality. It was
unostentatiously started upon its mission without fan-
fare. Quietly a few people gathered to consider the
merits of the idea of starting a work that at heart should
be missionary, assist Sunday schools as well as day
schools where the teachers were Christian, distribute
Bibles and religious tracts, and *care for orphans.*

At first the orphanage work was least in the thought of the founder, but it grew to be practically all-encompassing of his spiritual interest and prayer energy, so largely did it overshadow the other endeavors undertaken by the Institution.

The Institution was started solely with God as its Patron and never once did it veer from this original plan. Muller felt that God meant what he said when affirming *"the silver and gold are mine."* If the work was centered in the divine will, there would be plenty of God's silver and gold to promote its Christian interests.

"The Lord was the Banker of the Institution," writes Frederick Warne in his biography of Mr. Muller. "He knew all would be well. Slowly but surely the little institution grew. Faith and its heavenly response went hand in hand, and being weighted and borne down by no anxiety as to debt, as many religious agencies are, the trustful founder was able to give himself wholly to prayer for the means and grace to carry the work on."

The first report of the Institution covered the initial fifteen months. It was not a flourishing report, but was the spring from which a mighty river of influence was to go forth to water the parched harvest fields of the earth.

"It is now fifteen months," writes Mr. Muller in that report, "since, in dependence upon the Lord for the supply of means, we have been enabled to supply poor children with schooling, circulate the Holy Scriptures, and aid missionary labors. During this time, though the field of labor has been continually enlarged, and though we have . . . been brought low in funds, the Lord has never allowed us to be obliged to stop the

work. We have been enabled during this time to establish three day schools, and to connect with the
Institution two other charity day schools . . .

"In addition to this the expenses connected with a
Sunday school and an Adult school have been likewise defrayed, making seven schools altogether.

"The number of children that have thus been provided with school, in the day schools alone amounts
to 439. The number of copies of the Holy Scriptures
which have been circulated is 795 Bibles and 753 New
Testaments.

"We have also sent, in aid of Missionary labors in
Canada, in the East Indies and on the Continent of
Europe, £117 11s."

Year by year the blessing of the Lord was upon the
Institution and in response to Muller's prayers every
need was supplied. In the report of 1855, Mr. Muller
said that more than £7,204 was given for the support
of schools during the twenty-one years of its existence;
another £16,115, for missions. There had been a total
of 13,949 Bibles, 9,047 New Testaments distributed
at a cost of £3,389 10s. 1d.

*"Without any one having been personally applied
to for anything by me* the sum of £74,132 6s. was
given to me for the orphans *as a result of prayer to
God* from the commencement of the work up to May
26, 1855," Mr. Muller reports for that year.

Through the long years God richly supplied the
needs. In the Fifty-fourth Report of the Institution
for the year 1893, which was the fifty-ninth year of
the work, he says, "The readers of the last report will
remember under what particular trials we entered
upon the last financial year of the Institution . . . but
we trusted in God; and with unshaken confidence in

Him, and we expected that we should somehow or the other be helped. . . .

"While thus we went on my heart at peace habitually, being assured that all this was permitted by God, to prepare a blessing for thousands, who would afterward read the record of His dealings with us from May 26, 1892 to May 26, 1893."

During that year of trial on August 30, while reading Psalm 81:10, *"Open thy mouth wide, and I will fill it,"* Mr. Muller said, "Remembering the work of the Holy Spirit in my heart when reading this verse on December 5, 1835, and the effect which this had in leading me to found the greatest Orphan Institution in the world . . . putting the Bible aside I fell on my knees and asked God that He would graciously be pleased to repeat His former kindness, and to supply me again more abundantly with means. Accordingly in less than half an hour, I received £50 from a Bristol donor. . . . By the last delivery, at 9 p.m., . . . I had . . . £152 in all, this day, as the result of prayer."

In the last Report of the Institution which Mr. Muller ever gave, (for the year 1896-97) he goes into a detailed summary of the blessings of God upon the work since its founding. "This is the last record," writes Fred Warne in his biography, "which Mr. Muller penned of his stewardship, and he was fully assured that the fruit which he had been enabled to see was but little in comparison with what he should behold in the day of Christ's appearing."

We give this report in full that the reader might realize *how greatly God had filled Mr. Muller's mouth* since December 5, 1835, when God first gave him this wonderful promise in Psalms.

SCHOOLS

"In our various schools we have had from the beginning 121,683 pupils. In all these schools was more or less blessing; but in some very great blessing, so that the Christian teachers sometimes had to record the conversion of 50 or 60 pupils in one school during one half-year. Never have been other than truly converted teachers engaged, and constantly the blessing of God has been sought in their labors. Mr. Wright and I seek habitually the blessing of God on the schools, as well as on the other branches of the Institution.

"Also, when we meet with our fellow laborers for prayer, the schools of the Institution are habitually remembered in prayer. On the ground of the information which we received from the school inspectors of the Institution, and from the Christian masters and mistresses of the many schools founded and supported during the past 63 years, and also from the letters received from the pupils, after they have left the schools, we have reason to believe that, when the harvest of this world will be reaped at the last in full, we shall, out of these 121,683 pupils, meet tens of thousands in glory.

BIBLE DISTRIBUTION

"During the past 63 years there have been circulated by means of this Institution, in almost all parts of the world, and in many different languages, 281,652 Bibles, 1,448,662 New Testaments, 21,343 copies of the Book of Psalms, and 222,196 other portions of the Holy Scriptures. On this branch of the Institution the Lord's blessing has been asked day by day for sixty-three years; and the Lord has blessed this work most abundantly. In connection with very many Bible

Carriages in England, Ireland, Scotland, Spain, Australia and other countries, where the cheap Testaments are sold to the workers of these carriages at half-price, and Bibles at three-fourths of the price, God has granted most abundant blessing.

"In this way to the obscure villages has the Word of God been carried and made a blessing to multitudes. This has been especially the case among the Papists in Ireland. When it pleased God to open Spain, in the year 1868, I sought at once with thousands, yea, many thousands of copies, of the Holy Scriptures to enter into Spain; and it pleased God most abundantly to bless the simple reading of the Holy Scriptures in Spanish (which they had never seen in their whole life) to multitudes. And this has been going on in Spain ever since, more or less, viz., the Holy Scriptures have been circulated, and the Lord has caused His blessing to rest upon it.

"When Italy was opened for the preaching of the Truth and the circulation of the Holy Scriptures, it pleased the Lord to grant to me the great privilege to enter immediately into Italy with the Italian Bible and New Testament, in thousands of copies, and they were spread in all directions; and, in answer to our prayers, most abundantly were they blessed. It was not long after this that the Papal State, yea, even Rome itself, was opened for the circulation of the Holy Scriptures; yea, Rome, into which the Pope and the Popish Priests had not allowed a trunk, or portmanteau, or bag to be introduced without searching every package, to see whether there might be a Bible.

"Often even the pockets of visitors were searched, so that God's Holy Word might not enter the seat of the Papacy. These Bibles, New Testaments and portions of the Holy Scriptures were most abundantly blessed, and God allowed us abundantly to reap, and showed by the answers to prayer that we did not wait on Him in vain. Even recently we sent 2,600 New Testaments in Italian to Rome, and 550 Bibles.

"But the circulation of the Holy Scriptures has not been confined by us to the countries referred to, but in China, in the Straits of Malacca, particularly in Demerara and Essequibo, in Nova Scotia, and in France, we have sought to labor in this way; and in all these various countries it has pleased God most abundantly to answer our prayers and to allow us to see most abundant fruit as the result of our prayers.

"Our hearts are filled with gratitude when we remember the thousands of precious souls in Spain, Italy, France, Ireland, the Colonies of Australia, China, and in many hundreds of the spiritually dark villages of Great Britain that thus have been benefited. We have also been allowed, within the past sixty-three years, to gladden the hearts of thousands of aged poor persons in supplying them with a copy of the Holy Scriptures printed in large type, as the Bible they possessed was too small for their sight.

Missionary Operations

"During the past sixty-three years the Lord has also allowed us to seek to aid missionary operations in China, India, the Straits of Malacca, Palestine, Egypt, North Africa, South Africa, Central Africa, Demerara, Essequibo, Berbice, South America, the United States of America, Nova Scotia, Canada, Spain, Italy, France, Germany, Austria, Belgium, Armenia, Ireland, Scotland, Wales and in all the various spiritually-dark places of England. Several hundred missionaries have been, to a greater or less degree, aided with pecuniary supplies or otherwise. (On this subject and on the Mission schools, £259,776 17s. 10d. had been expanded up to May, 1897.)

"God has been besought on behalf of these, His servants, day by day, these sixty-three years, and it has pleased Him to allow us to reap and have most abundant answers to our prayers. When we received letters from these beloved servants of Christ, of which we have very many thousands, we again and again found not only that scores of persons had been converted, but even hundreds.

"This glorious work of winning these souls for our precious Lord Jesus, in connection with this Institution, has been more or less going on during the past sixty-three years, through the labor of these several hundred servants of Christ, and we do not hesitate to state that we have the fullest reason to believe that tens of thousands of souls have been brought to the knowledge of our Lord Jesus.

"I state also that from our own midst, as a church, sixty-three brethren and sisters have gone forth to foreign fields of labor, some of whom have finished their labor on earth; but there are forty-two yet engaged in this precious service. In China, in the East Indies, in the Straits, in British Guiana, in South Africa, in Central Africa, in North Africa, in Nova Scotia, Canada, the United States, in Egypt, in Spain, in Italy, in France, in Germany, in Ireland and England, the labors of these missionary brethren have been abundantly blessed.

TRACT DISTRIBUTION

"There have likewise been circulated in connection with this Institution more than 111 millions (minutely

111,489,067) of Scriptural books, pamphlets, and tracts. Notice, esteemed reader, not tens of thousands, not hundreds of thousands, merely, but above a hundred and eleven millions.

"We adore and praise God for the honor and privilege bestowed on us, thus to scatter the truth in many countries and in many different languages; but the most precious part is that in this way also thousands of precious souls have been blessed. Many hundred godly brethren and sisters in Christ have helped us in this precious service, to spread the truth everywhere; and, in many thousands of letters received, when fresh supplies of tracts or books were asked to be sent, the statements also were made how greatly those tracts and books, which had been sent to them gratuitously, had been owned of God.

Spiritual Blessing on the Orphan Work

"I come now, lastly, to the Orphan work, which likewise, during the sixty-one years of its existence, has been abundantly blessed. In all, during the thirty-one years, 2,813 orphans left the Institution as believers. In addition to this, we had information by letter or personal intercourse that many hundreds were brought to the knowledge of the Lord after they had left the Institution; and there are 609 orphans in the five houses, regarding whom the matrons, masters, and female teachers are united in judgment that they are regenerated. The reader will see by this how abundantly it has pleased the Lord to bless our labors to the orphans. One or other of the readers may be inclined to say, will these orphans who now profess to be believers continue in the ways of God? My reply is, 50 or 60 years ago a number of young orphans professed faith in the Lord Jesus, and, with a few exceptions, they walked in the fear of God, 20, 30, 40 years, till the Lord took them to Himself. There is still one of those living who has' now walked in the ways of God as a constant believer 58 years.

Money Received

"The total amount of money received, by prayer and faith, for the various objects of the Institution since March 5th, 1834, is one million four hundred and twenty-four thousand six hundred and forty-six pounds, six shillings and ninepence halfpenny (£1,424,646 6s. 9½d.)!"

Mr. Muller's faith was thus grandly rewarded, for God furnished in response to his prayers approximately seven and a half million dollars. From a most insignificant beginning the work grew until it became a leading supporter of missions, distributor of Bibles and religious literature, as well as the outstanding "father of the orphans." Had Mr. Muller done nothing but promote the Scriptural Knowledge Institution it would have been a work worthy of any life.

Orphans were so largely his passion that these other things were relegated to the background . . . a background of magnificent proportions. His was a life of dual service . . . sire of the Institution and of the orphanage.

CHAPTER XI

TRIALS OF FAITH

THE BUILDING of Mr. Muller's spiritual life was a constant conflict. While outwardly he displayed a calm attitude toward circumstances, inwardly he battled to obtain this seeming peace. During the earlier years of his faith pilgrimage his battles were more severe and came more often upon him to block that upward climb toward spiritual serenity. He laid the foundation for his prayer life by facing the obstacles in the way of communion with God.

A lack of prayer is more evident during the first years following his conversion than later, since the habit had to be builded by diligence. It was by no means an immediate acquisition with him. For instance, while yet a student at Halle, following his spiritual awakening, he decided to leave for the University of Berlin. At once the Spirit checked him for making up his mind with such a burst of speed and not seasoning it with prayer. He says, "When the morning came on which I had to apply to the university for testimonials, the Lord graciously stirred me up prayerfully to consider the matter."

After prayer he discovered that it was not God's will for him to make the change. While this was an insignificant incident, still it taught him that his decisions must not be made without carefully considering

114

them in the light of partnership with God. Later in his work there were to be many incidents where he was to be checked by the Lord in setting out on a certain course without first laying it before God.

His assurance that a course was right was founded upon this necessity, which he learned at Halle, of not undertaking an action without seasons of waiting upon God for His sanction.

At about this time, early in 1826, he learned another lesson which was to be used in toughening the fibre of his soul. That concerned itself with Bible reading. Being converted, he did not read his Bible, though he read about the Bible extensively. He was to master this lesson in faith's curriculum before God trusted him with many answers to his prayers.

"My difficulty in understanding it (the Bible), and the little enjoyment I had in reading it, made me careless in reading it . . ."

This was in 1826, but when sixteen years of his spiritual warfare had passed, he discovered that a radical change in the method of conducting the spiritual ministrations with his own soul brought added victories. His conflicts within and without were great. He writes, "Before this time my practice had been, at least for ten years previously, as an habitual thing to give myself to prayer after having dressed myself in the morning. Now I saw that the most important thing I had to do was to give myself to the reading of the Word of God, and to meditation on it, that my heart might be comforted, encouraged, warned, reproved."

Those prayer sessions, when he bared his soul to God, were times of confession. "The result is," he states, "that there is always a good deal of confession . . ."

When the London Society accepted him as a missionary, one of the conditions was that he would study with them for six months. This brought him great disappointment. In 1828, he assures us, "For a few moments, therefore, I was greatly disappointed and tried." These trials and discouragements, which circumstances and conditions brought him, were to be a constant companion of his entire Christian endeavor.

So great were his victories of faith that we are prone to believe that Mr. Muller was ever tried, and so many his answers to prayer that he was ever disappointed when the reply did not come shortly from God. Such is far from the truth.

On March 7, 1831, he says, "I was again tempted to disbelieve the faithfulness of the Lord, and though I was not miserable, still, I was not so fully resting upon the Lord that I could triumph with joy." He was in dire need and it seemed that God had forgotten him. Shortly however he assures us that joy returned with the answer to his cry in the form of a gift of five sovereigns.

Seven years later this same trial overwhelmed him. On September 17, 1838, he writes, "This evening I was rather tried respecting the long delay of larger sums coming. . . ." When he closed the following year he refers to "the trials of faith during the year," but adds, "Should it be supposed . . . by anyone in reading the details of our trials of faith during the year . . . that we have been disappointed in our expectations or discouraged in the work, my answer is . . . such days were expected from the commencement. . . . Our desire is not that we may be without trials of faith, but that the Lord graciously be pleased to support us in the trial."

He also refers to "the deeper trials of his faith," those things that really disturbed him and kept his mind wandering during seasons of meditation. This was a constant battle with him.

From these occasions of conflict he found release in going to his knees in prayer. "When other trials, still greater," he states, "but which I cannot mention, have befallen me . . . I poured out my soul before God, and arose from my knees in peace." This was his method of breaking Satan's hold upon his life in the hours of battle.

There were occasions when everything was dark in outlook. Not all was light, nor were all of his days free from those harassing conditions which Christians face. "When sometimes all has been dark, exceedingly dark . . . judging from natural appearances; yea, when I should have been overwhelmed indeed in grief and despair had I looked at things after the outward appearances . . . I have sought to encourage myself by laying hold in faith on God's almighty power, His unchangeable love, and His infinite wisdom."

A few years later he received a great disappointment when a letter arrived from a sister saying she was unable to send the large sums she had promised. Muller realized shortly that he had placed his trust in the promise of the lady and not in the promise of God. God spoke to him softly, he says, through the passage, "We know that all things work together for good to them that love God." Immediately peace was restored to his troubled soul.

Mr. Muller was anxious that none who read his "Narrative" or came into contact with God's dealings with him would think that he were not in spiritual need all the time. He refers to this being in constant need

more than twenty years after he first began to trust
God for his daily supplies. And these needs were not
merely of a financial nature — in fact, he had more
immediate freedom from financial worries, or present
victory over his heavy financial burdens than over his
other more personal "needs."

He was subject to constant temptation along lines
of appearing insincere, or of being proud over what
God had done through him.

He writes, under the stress of such spiritual problems often arising in his soul, "I am in continual need.
. . . If left to myself I should fall a prey to Satan.
Pride, unbelief or other sins would be my ruin. I cannot stand for a moment if left to myself. Oh, that
none of my readers might think that I could not be
puffed up by pride, and think of me as being beyond
unbelief. . . . No, I am as weak as ever." In 1848 he
added, "I need as much as ever to be upheld as to
faith and every other grace. I am therefore in 'need,'
in great 'need,' and therefore, dear Christian readers,
help me with your prayers."

To assure us that he was not beyond trial, he said,
"Straits and difficulties I expected from the beginning.
. . . Therefore the longer I go on in this service, the
greater the trials of one kind or another become."

He faced his weak moments as everyone does.
Though strong in faith still he felt the constant urge
to keep in instant touch with God, for otherwise, his
inner weaknesses would overcome him.

On May 13, 1837, he affirmed, "Today I have had
again much·reason to mourn over my corrupt nature,
particularly on account of want of gratitude for the
many temporal mercies by which I am surrounded.
I was so sinful as to be dissatisfied on account of the

dinner, because I thought it would not agree with me, instead of thanking God for rich provisions and asking *heartily* the Lord's rich blessing upon it. . . . I rejoice in the prospect of that day, when, seeing Jesus as He is, I shall be like Him."

He was often troubled by the many spiritual voids that marked his work. On October 7, 1833, he checked the results of his personal ministry by that of Mr. Craik. He said, "Many more were convinced of sin through brother Craik's preaching than my own. 1. Brother Craik is more spiritually minded than I am. 2. That he prays more earnestly for the conversion of sinners than I do. 3. He more frequently addresses himself to sinners than I do."

This led Mr. Muller to an instant study of his lack of concern for the sinner's welfare, and once he found the cause, he remedied it through special seasons of prayer in which he asked God for a deepened sense of the tragedy that dogs his path.

When he felt led to build Ashley Down as was his custom he weighed the arguments for and against such a course. Among the arguments against the action was the thought that his constant battle against pride might overwhelm him in the new undertaking. "I should be in danger of being lifted up," he wrote. "I should be in danger of it indeed. . . . I cannot say that hitherto the Lord has kept me humble. But I can say that hitherto He has given me a hearty desire to give Him all the glory. . . . I have to beseech the Lord that He be pleased to give me a lowly mind."

This prayer which moved him in 1851 was the result of constantly facing the many praises, which came from friends, because of the daily miracles his faith seemed to bring to pass.

Through the years he worried not a little about a tendency to become irritable because of his physical condition. During the first decade after his conversion he fought to overcome any slight indication that he was not pleased with how he felt, or how the weather might be, or whatever the soul-upheaving circumstances he was going through. An instance of this is found in his Journal under the entry of January 16, 1838.

"The weather has been cold," he says, "for several days, but today I suffered much, either because it was colder than before or because I felt it more owing to the weakness of my body . . . I arose from my knees and stirred the fire; but I still remained very cold . . . I was a little irritated by this. At last, having prayed for some time, I was obliged to rise and take a walk. . . . I now entreated the Lord that this circumstance might not be permitted to rob me of the precious communion which I had with Him the last three days, for this was the object at which Satan aimed. I confessed also my sin of irritability on account of the cold and sought to have my conscience cleansed through the blood of Jesus. He had mercy upon me, my peace was restored . . . and I had uninterrupted communion with Him."

In 1844 he wrote, "I desired more power over my besetting sins." When one reads the few times in which Mr. Muller tells the story of his battle over irritability, he is led to wonder if this was not one of those troublesome sins which constantly nagged at his soul.

His entire life was checkered with afflictions, irritations, trials and the victory of peace and spiritual repose. When his daughter took typhus fever in 1854, this checkering appears in his Journal, where he writes:

"Now was the trial of faith. But faith triumphed. . . . While I was in this affliction, this great affliction, besides being at peace as far as the Lord's dispensation was concerned, I also felt perfectly at peace with regard to the cause of the affliction. . . . It was the Father's rod, applied in infinite wisdom and love for the restoration of my soul from a state of lukewarmness.

"Conscious as I was of my manifold weaknesses, failings and shortcomings, so that I too would be ready to say with the Apostle Paul, 'O wretched man that I am!' yet I was assured that this affliction was . . . for the trial of my faith."

He found this route of peace through affliction early in his Christian life. As far back as in 1829 he writes, "The weaker I became in body, the happier I was in my spirit." This was during a severe illness on May 15 when he despaired of living.

"Never in my whole life," he continues, "had I seen myself so vile, so guilty, so altogether what I ought not to have been as at this time. It was as if every sin of which I had been guilty was brought to my remembrance; but at the same time I could realize that all my sins have been completely forgiven. . . . The result of this was great peace."

One of the last entries he made in his Journal shows this same checkering of the divine will in his life. On March 1, 1898, shortly before his death, he wrote, "For about 21 months with scarcely the least intermission *the trial of our faith and patience has continued.* Now, today, the Lord has *refreshed* my heart." The occasion of this blessing was receiving a legacy for approximately $7,500.

Mr. Muller had learned the simple lesson that how-

ever great the affliction, God in His kind providence
would not forsake him—provided he remained stead-
fast in faith and relied greatly upon secret prayer.

The key to his spiritual victories, whatever the nature of the soul depression, is found in an entry on
June 25, 1835. He says, "These last three days I
have had very little real communion with God, and
have therefore been very weak spiritually, and have
several times felt irritability of temper." The following day he wrote, "I was enabled, by the grace of
God, to rise early, and I had nearly two hours in
prayer before breakfast. I now feel this morning
more comfortable."

It was prayer that swept his soul free of doubt, dis-
temper and the after-effects of a trial by the incoming
tide of peace. For this reason he could make such
remarks as this entry on March 9, 1847, "The *greater*
the difficulties, the *easier for faith.*" And a later one,
"The greater the trial, the sweeter the victory."

Mr. Muller decried any evidence of having the *gift
of faith.* He had faith, as any Christian may have it,
but not that peculiar gift of which Paul speaks in
I Corinthians 12:9.

"Think not, dear reader," he writes, "that I have the
gift of faith . . . which is mentioned along with 'the
gifts of healing,' 'the working of miracles' . . . and
that on that account I am able to trust in God. . . . If
I were only one moment left by myself my faith would
utterly fail. . . . It is not true that my faith is that gift
of faith. . . . It is the self-same faith which is found in
every believer . . . for little by little it has been in-
creasing for the last six and twenty years."

In charting the results of this marvelous life of
trust, the speed with which he obtained multiplied

thousands of answers to his prayers, we must be careful not to remove Mr. Muller from the realm of the thoroughly human. He is anxious to have his readers think of him in the same light as they do of themselves. He possessed no character traits nor divine possessions, not within the reach of every believer.

The trials which blocked his spiritual advancement were those common to every Christian. The human tempers, the frailties of his body, mind and spirit were those which mark true members of God's kingdom. His victories came through prayer, trust in the Lord's unfailing promises and faith that God's truth could not fail; and if he thus achieved, he would have us also see that similar faith victories are within our reach.

There is only one route to soul repose . . . and that is the highway that leads to God's throne, *prayer.*

"It is not enough to begin to pray," he advises us, "nor to pray aright; nor is it enough to continue *for a time* to pray; but we must patiently, believingly continue in prayer, until we obtain an answer; and further, we have not only to *continue* in prayer unto the end, but we have also to *believe* that God does hear us and will answer our prayers. Most frequently we fail *in not continuing* in prayer until the blessing is obtained, and in not expecting the blessing."

Chapter XII

GIFTS AND GIVING

THE SUM total of Mr. Muller's life was giving. He gave himself in prayer that in return God might give the necessary supplies, not only for his own family, but also for the large family of orphans. Basing his life upon receiving from God, in return he practiced the art of liberality. Since God gave to him through faith he must also be among those who were faithful givers.

Even the texts that influenced him most were those on giving and receiving. Throughout his "Narrative" you will find these passages boldly across the pages. Early he and his wife were led to that scripture, *"Sell that ye have and give alms"* (Luke 12:33). This was to be the course of their lives. They were to be sellers and givers.

The Lord, speaking through His Word, said, *"Whatsoever ye shall ask in my name, that will I do . . ."* (John 14:13). And Mr. Muller based his work upon this promise, asking largely that the Father might be glorified.

Since God had told him to open his mouth Mr. Muller never feared to ask for whatever his work must have. To him this promise was the foundation of all spiritual and temporal success. Like a bird, he opened his mouth and the Lord filled it with the supply of all financial needs.

In Genesis he loved the name Jehovah Jirah, for it meant *the Lord will provide* (Genesis 22:14). Grandly did God give the provisions for the Institution and his Orphan Houses.

From the first records of Mr. Muller's donations, we find him giving on a large scale. During the first year of his life of trust (1831) he received £151 in answer to prayer; but he gave away £50 of that sum. During the second year he gave £70 out of an income of £195. His income for 1833 was £267 brought in through faith, and his gifts amounted to £110.

This giving and receiving kept pace with each other during the long years of his career. For the ten years from 1836 to 1845 his income from all sources was approximately £3,400 and through faith he placed back into the Lord's work about £1,280. During the following decade his yearly income was about £500 and for the same time he gave over half of this sum away. His gifts for that decade amounted to £2,660.

From 1856 to 1865 his income amounted to £10,670, over $50,000 a year; and out of this he devoted £8,250, or a total sum of $41,250, to God's work. Out of £20,500, received from 1866 to 1875, he turned back to Christian endeavors, nearly an average of £1,800 a year. During the next ten years, the last of which a direct record is available, he gave away £22,330 from an income of £26,000, which left him the sum of £3,670 to live on for a period of ten years, or a little over $1,800 a year. And it must be remembered that this decade—1876 to 1885—was devoted to extensive missionary travels, which constituted a heavy drain on his personal finances.

These donations came to him through faith alone, and he recognized that he must be the channel through which God's gifts should flow out to others in need. He looked upon himself as the Lord's steward. What money he received he believed should be given rather than hoarded.

A crippled woman, who through the years was a constant though a small giver to the orphanage work, expressed Mr. Muller's philosophy of *living* and *giving*. She began giving a penny a week out of her earnings toward the care of the orphans, and the Lord blessed her so much that she was able to raise her weekly gift to six shillings, or a dollar and a half. One gift she wrapped in a piece of paper, on which she had written: *"Give; give; give—be ever giving. If you are living, you will be giving. Those who are not giving are not living."*

The total amount Mr. Muller gave away out of his private funds amounted to approximately $180,000 from the year 1831 to November, 1877. This it must be recalled came out of a poor trustful man's penury. He had only what he prayed in from day to day.

The Fifty-ninth Report of the Institution, issued May 26, 1898, immediately after Mr. Muller's death, reveals a very interesting item concerning this servant's method of giving. Year by year in the annual Reports there were frequent entries of gifts *"from a servant of the Lord Jesus, who, constrained by the love of Christ, seeks to lay up treasure in heaven."*

Mr. Wright, who succeeded Mr. Muller as head of the Institution, checked those entries, and found that this servant had given up to March 1, 1898, the aggregate sum of *eighty-one thousand four hundred and ninety pounds, eighteen shillings and eightpence.*

That servant was none other than Mr. Muller himself, who gave out of his own money more than sixty-four thousand five hundred pounds to the Scriptural Knowledge Institution alone, and to other individuals and organizations seventeen thousand more. It seems inconceivable that a poor man should thus give more than $407,450 to the work of God.

There is no other case on record of such magnificent gifts coming from a humbled servant of the Lord. It is estimated that John Wesley gave away nearly $150,000 to spread the cause of Christianity. When Wesley died he left behind him *a well-worn frock coat, two silver teaspoons—and the Methodist Church.*

When Mr. Muller died his entire personal estate amounted to £169 9s. 4d., approximately $850, of which his household effects, books, furniture, etc., amounted to well over $500. The only money in his possession was actually about $350. He died a poor man, though the Lord had entrusted to his hands well over a half-million dollars.

George Muller looked upon himself as God's steward. One of the texts which influenced him was, *"Give and it shall be given unto you. Good measure pressed down, shaken together and running over shall men give unto your bosom."*

He believed and saw this promise bountifully verified. "I had *given*," he testified, "and God caused to be *given to me again* and bountifully."

He affirms that he believed what he read in the Bible, and acted accordingly. Though acting on God's promises, and rejecting the offer of a stated salary of £55 a year, God literally gave him a fortune . . . a fortune which he shared with those in need.

Out of this overflow of experience in giving, Mr.

Muller had very definite thoughts on giving. Giving to him was the heart of the Christian life . . . give self in full surrender to God, and out of what God gives return to Him liberal gifts. This was his giving philosophy. Let us read and heed some of his advice on this subject.

"Many of the children of God," he affirms, "lose in a great measure the privilege, and also the blessing to their own souls, of communicating to the Lord's work to the necessities of the poor, for want of *a regular habit of giving*."

When asked, "How shall I give?" Mr. Muller responded:

"1. Seek to keep before you that the Lord Jesus Christ has redeemed us, and that . . . we are not our own, because *we are bought with a price.* . . . All then that we have belongs to Him, and we have to look on our possessions as a faithful steward. . . .

"2. The *habitual* using of our means, the *regularly* communicating as the Lord prospers us, is next to be attended to. As far as practicable, we should seek to do this weekly, according to the word—'Upon the first day of the week let every one of you lay by him in store as God hath prospered him' (I Cor. 16:2) . . .

"3. Every one should do so. . . .

"4. With regard to the amount to be given, no rule can be laid down, because what we ought to do should not be done in a legal spirit, but from love and gratitude to the Blessed One Who died for us."

On the score of the method of giving, Mr. Muller was often asked, "How shall I put aside my gifts? Must I actually separate this money from my other money?"

"That is the simplest," he answered, "and in many

respects the best way. . . . A memorandum book may be kept, in which on one side is entered what is put aside for the Lord, to be expended on the poor, or for other benevolent and religious purposes, and on the other side may be put down what has been expended, and from time to time a balance may be struck. The amount thus put aside for the Lord is of course faithfully to be used for Him, else it would be mocking God; and therefore, instead of obtaining a blessing, it would rather be a curse."

"Am I to give with the idea of being repaid by the Lord?" a friend asked this man of prayer.

"Though we should never give," he responded, *"for the sake of being repaid by the Lord,* still, this will be the case, if we give from right motives. It is God's own declaration that it will be so. This is plainly to be gathered from the following passages . . . 'Give, and it shall be given unto you.' . . . 'He that hath pity on the poor, lendeth unto the Lord; and that which he hath given will He pay him again.' "

This giving, Mr. Muller was careful to explain, must be to the Lord and not unto man. Man may be the recipient, but with a humble heart gifts must be scattered abroad, not for the praise of man, but for the blessings of God upon the giver's body and soul.

From his own experience and through the many letters he received he was well able to give testimony as to the blessing which comes from systematic giving.

"I enclose a Post Office Order for £5," writes an Irish manufacturer, "which by the blessing of Almighty God, I am enabled to send you this year. You will no doubt remember that the first sum I sent to you was 5s., I think now four years ago; and, indeed at that time it was a large sum for me to send. . . .

"For some years previous to the time I sent you the first amount I was at times much perplexed over the subject of giving; and the end of my reasoning was always that a person so straitened in circumstances as I was then, was not called upon to give. I kept this opinion until one of your Reports fell into my hands, and from the accounts contained therein, was encouraged to send you the first amount of 5s. *Soon after I thought my circumstances got somewhat easier.* . . . I have proved that just as I give the Lord gives in return. . . . I sometimes withheld when I ought not, and just as I withheld, the Lord in His infinite mercy withheld also. . . . But above all, I have to thank God that my spiritual condition is much improved since I began to give."

"Since I began to devote a regular proportion of my earnings to the cause of God," wrote a donor from Orkney, whose gift amounted to $15, "He has, I rejoice to say, greatly increased both my ability and desire to do so."

One man sent Mr. Muller a Paisley shawl, worth about $25, and with the gift enclosed a note, saying, "It is now about ten years since I first adopted the principle of proportionate giving. . . . Prior to that I used to wonder, with every sovereign I gave, whether I was not doing more than was prudent, and the result was I had little pleasure in giving. Now, however, having been greatly prospered in business, I find myself able to give fourfold what I did, and can understand better what is meant by the blessedness of giving. . . . The adoption of the principle of proportionate giving has enabled me on the one hand to guide my affairs with discretion, and on the other to refrain from 'robbing God.' "

Mr. Muller was a stickler for obtaining gifts in God's way. "It is not enough," he says, "to obtain means for the work of God, but that these means should be obtained in God's way. To ask unbelievers for means is not God's way; to press even believers to give is not God's way; but the duty and the privilege of being allowed to contribute to the work of God should be pointed out, and this should be followed up with earnest prayer, believing prayer, and will result in the desired end."

This is a plan which he practiced throughout his life. Not once, even when asked to do so, did he ever tell anyone how pressing or how great were the needs. He always told this to the Lord, and expected God to move upon someone to supply those needs.

He often thought that giving in adversity would prove a greater blessing than giving in prosperity. Giving in adversity, when needs were pressing, shows that one truly trusts in God for supplying his daily needs, while giving in prosperity places upon the giver no particular hardship.

He never hoarded, for when one hoards, he affirms, God would send him to his laid-up treasures rather than to his knees in the time of need. "I have every reason to believe," he testifies, "that, had I begun to lay up, the Lord would have stopped the supplies. . . . Let no one profess to trust in God, and yet lay up for the future wants, otherwise the Lord will first send him to the hoard he has amassed, before he can answer the prayer for more."

Even to the smallest items, Mr. Muller believed that he was God's steward. He did not think that he owned, or possessed anything only as they came as gifts from the Lord to be used for God's service.

"It is the Lord's order," he observes, "that, in whatever way He is pleased to make us His stewards, whether as to temporal or spiritual things, if we are indeed acting as stewards and not as owners, he will make us stewards over more. . . .

"Even in this life, as to temporal things, the Lord is pleased to repay those who act for Him as stewards. . . . But how much greater is the spiritual blessing we receive, both in this life and in the life to come, if constrained by the love of Christ, we act as God's stewards, respecting that with which He is pleased to intrust us."

God richly supplied Mr. Muller with donations of all kinds and descriptions. Money was sent in from practically every possible source and of all types. Some gifts were large, running into the thousands of dollars, and others were for a penny. Some sent bread, others shoes. Some felt constrained of the Lord to sell articles of furniture and give the money to Mr. Muller for his orphans. Jewelry by the thousands of dollars worth was sent to be sold for the work.

Autographs were given to be sold, as that of William IV, and Sir Robert Peel. One man sent a silver medal which he had won in helping take Java in battle. Another delivered a horse-car to be disposed of, and a lady sent some of her original hymns to be published for the benefit of the orphans.

When needs were pressing, Mr. Muller would call the staff together for prayer, and often on getting off their knees, dray wagons would be seen backing up to the kitchen door, loaded with buns, bread, apples, cakes, potatoes, boxes of soap, sacks of peas, haunches of venison, rabbits and pheasants, and every other conceivable edible article.

During the last year of Mr. Muller's life among the gifts recorded were 7,203 quarterns of bread; 5,222 buns, 306 cakes; 44,669 pounds of apples; 40 sacks of potatoes; 20 boxes of soap; 9 tons of coal; 26 haunches of venison; 112 rabbits; 312 pheasants; 5 bags of oatmeal; 26 cases of oranges; 5 boxes of dates; and 4,013 pounds of meat, along with hundreds of other items.

From the time when Mr. Muller received the first gift of a shilling from a poor missionary to start the orphanage until he made one of his last entries in his Journal on March 1, 1898, God sent from all types of persons gifts small and great to carry on the work.

On March 1, 1898, he wrote, "For about 21 months with scarcely the least intermission the trial of our faith and patience has continued. Now, today, the Lord has refreshed our heart. This afternoon came in, for the Lord's work, £1,427 1s. 7d., as part payment of a legacy of the late Mrs. E. C. S. For 3 years and 10 months this money had been in the Irish Chancery Court. Hundreds of petitions had been brought before the Lord regarding it, and now at last, this portion of the total legacy has been received."

His first legacy, from a sick lad who died shortly afterwards, was for the sum of six shillings, sixpence, halfpenny, received on September 15, 1837. In between these two legacies were thousands of gifts.

In May, 1842, a gold watch was sent to the orphanage, with a note, saying, "A pilgrim does not want such a watch as this to make him happy; one of an inferior kind will do to show how swiftly time flies, and how fast he is hastening on to that Canaan where time will be no more."

A hotel proprietor sent 15s. 10d., representing a

penny a night per bed for each visitor during the quarter. One person sent £2 16s., as a tenth of the rent received "as promised to God." A commercial traveler wrote Mr. Muller enclosing £4 16s. which he had saved by traveling third class. One man about to be married sent $10 in thanks to God for His mercies while being single.

A man lost half of his property, and was led to send Mr. Muller $500 as a thank offering because God had spared the other half of his property. A friend sold pickles and made $3 which immediately he sent to Mr. Muller as a gift for the care of the orphans.

One person, after cutting down a tree and selling it, sent the Home £5 17s., from the sale of the wood. A little boy found a ring and on delivering it to its rightful owner, he received a shilling, which he took to Mr. Muller as his gift. A miner lay dying one day, and all he had left was a little gold dust which he at once caused to be dispatched to the orphanage.

A lady, being condemned for wearing earrings, sold them and gave the Institution the proceeds, amounting to $5. A poor widow died, and when her possessions were carefully gone through, a shilling was found in an envelope addressed to Mr. Muller as her last gift. A friend of the Home gave up smoking one year, and at the end of that time sent Mr. Muller $100, "a gift representing what I have saved by not smoking during this year."

God gave a fisherman a good herring catch one night and immediately he sent Mr. Muller $15 to be used for the Home, as a token of heaven's blessings. A hunter one season decided to forego his usual hunting trip, the license for which amounted to $15, and instead he sent the money to the Home. "This way of spending it is more pleasing to the Master," he wrote.

A commercial traveler decided not to insure against railway accidents and sent the same premium money amounting to £2 to the Institution.

One day Muller received a letter enclosing $15 saying, "I have never lost an article, although my premises are so situated that they might be easily entered at night, thus showing how the Lord watches over those who trust in Him." The gift represented the money which a watch dog would have cost. Another person sent $25 "instead of keeping a dog, in the hope that some poor heathen may be brought to the knowledge of the Saviour."

Many gifts came as thank offerings for calamities which were averted. A veterinary surgeon, while attending a sick horse, had given it up for dead, but after he had prayed the animal recovered, so he sent Mr. Muller a gift. Another person, who broke his left arm, sent a small gift in thanks to God that he had not broken his *right* arm, or some more vital part such as his neck.

One father made it a practice of giving to the Home the exact amount it would require to care for an orphan each time a child was born in his family. This continued until the man was supporting seven children at home and seven children at Ashley Down.

A farmer sent a note to Mr. Muller with a gift of $5 saying, "Our heavenly Father has given us 34 chickens, and not one of them has been taken by the fox, although our neighbors have lost many."

The gifts were too many to enumerate them all, but they were prompted by every possible circumstance. Many restored thefts committed years earlier. Some thanked God for His blessings upon their married life. Not a few manufacturers gave a small gift for each article sold during a specified period. Others gave thank offerings for stolen or lost property recovered.

In 1851 Mr. Muller received a gift of $1.25, with the text, "Open thy mouth wide, and I will fill it." That evening he entered in his Journal, "My mouth has been filled, according to that portion of the Holy Scriptures sent me this morning. I have received this evening the sum of £3,000, being the largest donation I have had as yet."

Thus from year to year did God supply the needs out of thousands of bountiful storehouses which were consecrated to his work. When a need existed Mr. Muller would pray diligently for it, and shortly near by or thousands of miles distant, God would put it in the heart of some person to supply it. For more than sixty-three years God matched every petition of Mr. Muller with its appropriate gift.

Chapter XIII

THE EVENING OF HIS LIFE

After the missionary tours closed in May, 1892, Mr. Muller devoted himself mainly to caring for the Scriptural Knowledge Institution. He assumed as large a burden for the work as ever, though the heavy end rested mainly upon Mr. Wright's shoulders. As an old man, he was an active servant in his Master's vineyard.

There was his congregation at Bethesda to be looked after. This congregation had grown from the original seven Christians who met on a memorable evening in 1832 to form a church of ten churches now with a membership of more than 1,200. Out of the original church had sprung ten others, six of which were independent of the mother church, and four being affiliated with it.

Mr. Muller took turns with others in preaching on Sunday mornings to the several congregations, but Sunday evenings he preached mainly at Bethesda, where he usually addressed large audiences. He was also faithful in attending the various prayer meetings as time afforded. Occasionally he was invited to speak outside of Bristol, though he did not make these into extended preaching tours as formerly.

He was an active, happy old man, whose pleasure

137

was found in caring for the work of the Lord. More and more he gave himself to his chief delight, that of reading the Bible and while meditating upon it, bringing his petitions to the Lord. During the latter years of his life he read the Bible through four times yearly.

In his sermons he spoke with the vigor of a younger man. A. T. Pierson heard him speak on Sunday morning March 22, 1896, in the Bethesda Chapel. This was in his ninety-first year, "but there was a freshness, vigor and terseness in his preaching that gave no indication of failing powers; in fact, he had never seemed more fitted to express and impress the thoughts of God," writes Mr. Pierson.

In his younger years he was often ill, but these spells seemed to leave him as he advanced in age. In 1837 he feared he should go insane, so great was the pressure in his head, and often his stomach gave him severe trouble. In his ninety-second year he wrote in his Report, "I have been able every day, and all the day, to work, and that with ease as seventy years since."

When called upon to speak to the largest audiences during his missionary tours and on returning home to the Bethesda congregation he had no difficulty whatsoever.

On his ninetieth birthday, when he spoke to the Bethesda congregation, he remarked that his voice and chest were stronger than when he commenced preaching sixty-nine years earlier.

"His mental powers too were as clear as when he passed his examinations," writes Fred Warne. "For sixty-nine years and ten months he had been a happy man. That he attributed to two things. Firstly, he had maintained a good conscience, not wilfully going on a course he knew to be contrary to the mind of God. . . . Secondly, to his love of the Holy Scriptures."

He was a greater lover of the Bible at ninety than at thirty. It grew upon him with age. In it he found his supreme pleasure and daily he waited upon the Lord as the Word spoke to him.

During these last years, as he had been throughout his long life, he was a hard worker. He always arose at an early hour, spending several hours with the Bible, and at eight he went through his correspondence. After this he received his assistants and laid out much of their work.

In 1892 a reporter from the *Christian Commonwealth,* who had called upon Mr. Muller, wrote, "I was prepared to see a venerable-looking gentleman, bent beneath the weight of years, and physically feeble. To my surprise I found Mr. Muller in appearance a man of considerable bodily vigor. His tall, stately form was, as far as I observed, not in the least bowed by age, and when he afterwards accompanied me along the corridor his step was firm and his stride lengthy and rapid. His face wears an expression of austerity, and his strongly-marked features show that he is . . . a man of iron. Yet he knows how to smile, and when he does this, you see quite another aspect of his nature. . . . His manners are those of a prince. He speaks with great deliberation, with a noticeable German accent.

"Here is a man 87 years of age still carrying on with his own hand certainly one of the most remarkable organizations in the history of the world. An idea of the extent of his work may be gathered from the fact that he has, so he told me, seven assistants for correspondence alone."

Nor were those last years easy. There were heavy burdens to be borne. The trials of faith were as great as ever. On March 1, 1893, as an example of his difficulties, he entered in his Journal, "The income during this week was £92 8s. 8d., for the Orphans, and £9 11s. 2d. for the other objects; being about the sixth part of our weekly expenses; but now the great trial of our faith was nearly brought to a close, as will presently be seen."

Three days later, he wrote, "This very day God begins to answer our prayers, as we have received a very good offer for the land we have to sell, even £1,000 an acre. The beginning of the day was darker as to outward appearances than ever: but we trusted in God for help."

Mr. Muller received a heavy blow when his wife died on January 13, 1895. While he was to miss her, there was no evidence of loneliness to be displayed; for he found comfort in his daily communing with God for the needs of the Institution. The heavenly Father stood by his side through this great trial.

He preached the funeral of his second wife, as he had of his first. Seldom does a man of ninety conduct such a service. The faith that sustained him in other trials upheld him in this one also.

"I had an opportunity on last Friday," writes one who attended the funeral, "of attending the funeral services of Mrs. Muller . . . and witnessing a simple ceremony, which, perhaps was unique in the history of the world. Here the venerable and venerated patriarch conducted the whole service, and at the age of ninety seemed full of grand faith which has enabled him to accomplish so much and support him in all vicissitudes, trials and labors of a long life. . . .

"His faith seemed unmoved by trial, undimmed by age, and proof against the keenest bereavement. . . . He seemed independent of all the outside means which so many now deem essential to worship. Here we have an object lesson on faith by a man who has erected on Ashley Down such splendid monuments of his belief."

The following year when Mr. A. T. Pierson was holding meetings in Bristol, he asked Father Muller, as he called him, to speak at the closing meeting of the series, "and he did so, delivering a powerful address of forty-five minutes on Prayer in connection with Missions, and giving his own life-story in part, with a vigor of voice and manner that seemed a denial of his advanced age."

Toward the close of his life, doctors advised Mr. Muller to preach only once on Sunday, so accordingly he spoke usually in the morning services at Bethesda Chapel. Mr. Pierson, who heard him preach on March 22, 1896, at the Chapel, said, "He spoke on the 77th Psalm; of course he found here his favorite theme—prayer; and, taking that as a fair specimen of his average preaching, he was certainly a remarkable expositor of the Scripture even at ninety-one years of age."

In the autumn of 1897 he was invited to attend the Birmingham meeting of the British and Foreign Bible Society. Due to an indisposition, he asked to be excused from attending, saying, "Will you have the kindness to read to the meeting that I have been for 68 years and 3 months, viz., since July, 1829, a lover of the Word of God, and that uninterruptedly. During that time I have read considerably more than 100 times through the whole of the Old and New Testaments, with prayer and meditation, four times every year."

It is estimated that he read the Bible through more than two hundred times, one hundred of these times being, as he here suggests, on his knees.

"My great love for the Word of God," the letter continues, "and my deep conviction of the need of its being spread far and wide, have led me to pray to God to use me as an instrument to do this, and to supply me with means for it; and He has condescended to enable me to circulate the Scriptures in all parts of the earth, and in various languages; and has been pleased thus, simply through reading of the Holy Scriptures, to bring thousands of persons to the knowledge of the Lord Jesus."

But to all lives there must come an end, and this grand old man of faith was nearing that time. For him it was literally light at eventide. His days were to end simply and graciously. Like Enoch he walked with God, and "he was not, for God took him."

In the summer of 1897, the heat was trying, and he was set aside from labors through a short illness. His condition, thought to be critical, soon improved and he was able to be about his usual duties, preaching once a Sunday, attending a few prayer meetings, and overseeing with Mr. Wright the needs of the Home.

On Sunday morning prior to his death, he preached at the Alma Road Chapel. Then at evening he preached again at his beloved home church, the Bethesda Chapel, at which he had ministered for 66 years. His text was from II Corinthians 5:1, *"For we know that if our earthly house of this tabernacle were dissolved, we have a building of God, an house not made with hands, eternal in the heavens."*

This proved to be a gracious service, attended with the usual quiet of the Lord's leadership, and the text was rightly selected and fittingly so to close a long life of Christian labors.

On the following Monday evening, March 7, 1898, he attended the weekly prayer meeting at Bethesda Chapel, and greeted all of his friends with his customary geniality. On Wednesday he received at Orphan House No. 3 two friends from the National Free Church Conference then in session at Bristol.

Mr. Muller would never allow anyone personally to attend him during the night. Only when a doctor was needed would he permit such medical care. But on this Wednesday morning in speaking with Mr. Wright, he told him that he felt a weakness, saying when he arose that morning he had to rest several times while dressing.

Mr. Wright suggested that he ought to have someone in constant attendance on him and God's grand old man replied that possibly this would be a good suggestion.

An hour or so later, when Mr. Wright saw him again, Muller said, "The weakness has passed away; I feel quite myself again."

"You ought to take a longer rest in the morning," suggested Mr. Wright. But Mr. Muller pointed out how heavy the correspondence was, and thought that this would be impossible, for he always looked after the correspondence himself.

Mr. Wright proposed that he himself arrive at the Orphan Homes earlier to meet any emergencies that might arise. He added, "Suppose I begin tomorrow morning."

"We will say nothing about tomorrow," Mr. Muller replied with a deprecatory gesture.

That evening he conducted prayer meeting at the Institution as his custom was. He gave out the hymn, beginning:

> *The countless multitude on High*
> *Who tune their songs to Jesus' name,*
> *All merit of their own deny,*
> *And Jesus' worth alone proclaim.*

The last hymn he ever sang, as far as any one knows, was this, sung as a benediction to the service,

> *We'll sing of the Shepherd that died,*
> *That died for the sake of the flock;*
> *His Love to the utmost was tried,*
> *And immovable stood as a rock.*

When he bade his son-in-law good-night there was no sign of declining strength. He seemed to the last the vigorous old man he had always been and retired to rest as usual. Mr. Wright suggested that he have a night-attendant and Mr. Muller consented to such an arrangement "after tonight." He was never more to need human attention.

The following morning, March 10, a servant went to his room with a cup of tea, as was the custom. On knocking at the door there was no response, so she opened the door and found Mr. Muller lying on the floor. For some time as body strength began to wane, Mr. Muller asked for a glass of milk and a biscuit to be placed on his dressing table. "Whilst eating the biscuit, he was, it is surmised, seized with a fainting fit, from which he never recovered, and in falling he must have clutched at the table, for the cloth was disarranged and various articles were found scattered upon the floor," says Fred Warne in his biography.

His doctor was summoned, who thought possibly that Mr. Muller had been dead an hour or so.

"Dear old Mr. Muller," exclaimed a friend when the news reached him. "He just slipped quietly off Home as the gentle Master opened the door and whispered, 'Come.'"

His death even at such an old age produced a world-wide sensation. The spiritual forces created by his godly life of trust had reached the earth's ends. From across the waters toward the sunrise and the sunset came a responsive heart beat of sympathy. People were stirred when the news went forth by telegraph and cable from land to land that George Muller was dead. He was measured by no denominational bonds for he belonged to the whole Church and the entire world. The race sustained a loss in his death.

The golden chain of prayer that Mr. Muller's life of trust had woven finally was snapped. God, he estimated, had answered over fifty thousand of his prayers, many thousands of which were answered on the day he made them and often before he arose from his knees. Some of his petitions, however, lingered across the decades. Here is a sample of such asking . . .

"In November, 1844, I began to pray for the conversion of five individuals. I prayed every day without a single intermission, whether sick or in health, on the land or on the sea, and whatever the pressure of my engagements might be. Eighteen months elapsed before the first of the five was converted. I thanked God and prayed on for the others. Five years elapsed, and then the second was converted. I thanked God for the second, and prayed on for the other three. Day by day I continued to pray for them, and six years passed before the third was converted. I thanked God for the

three, and went on praying for the other two. These
two remained unconverted.

"The man to whom God in the riches of his grace
has given tens of thousands of answers to prayer in
the self-same hour or day in which they were offered
has been praying day by day for nearly thirty-six years
for the conversion of these individuals, and yet they
remain unconverted. But I hope in God, I pray on,
and look yet for the answer. They are not converted
yet, *but they will be.*"

This was the faith that carried him through every
straitened place. He met emergencies by asking and
in due time God supplied whatever the need might be.

Those prayers? you ask. In 1897, those two men,
sons of a friend of Mr. Muller's youth, were not converted, after he had entreated God in their behalf
for fifty-two years daily. But after his death God
brought them into the fold! Such was this man's
triumphant faith, whatever the difficulty. If God answered his prayer immediately, he thanked him. If
not, he kept on importuning the Lord until the response
came. That voice of prayer was now stilled.

The funeral took place on Monday, March 14, and
was a popular tribute of affection. A brief service was
held at Orphan House No. 3, where over a thousand
children met, for the last time to look into the face
of the father they had lost. The casket of plain elm,
without drapery of flowers, stood before a desk in the
spacious dining room, and Mr. Wright conducted the
service, speaking on Mr. Muller's life and labors.

Among those attending was an old lady who called
to see the man who in her youth had befriended her.
She was one of the first orphans to be received in the
Girls' Home on Wilson Street, sixty years before.

There were four present who walked from Wilson Street to the new Ashley Down house on moving day in June, 1849 with the other inmates of the Institution.

Slowly the procession formed in front of Ashley Down and thousands entered it to walk or drive in carriages to the Bethesda Chapel. His staff of workers, the elders and deacons in his churches, deputations from forty or fifty religious bodies, and thousands of friends marched in stately file to perform the last rights to this man to whom they owed a valuable lesson in faith.

At the chapel every available space was taken and scores were forced to remain outside. The hymns were sung which Mr. Muller had given out in his last prayer meeting and Mr. Wright spoke on the text, *"Jesus Christ, the same yesterday and today and forever."*

"He was wont to say to the young believers," Mr. Wright declared, " 'Put your finger on the passage on which your faith rests,' and he himself had read the Bible from end to end nearly two hundred times. He fed on the Word and was therefore strong. . . .

"I have been asked again and again lately as to whether the orphan work would go on. *It is going on!* Since the commencement of the year we have received between forty and fifty fresh orphans. . . . The other four objects of the Institution, according to the ability God gives, are still being carried on. . . . I cannot think, however, that the God Who has so blessed the work for so long will leave our prayers as to the future unanswered."

After the service, the procession re-formed and went to the Arno Vale Cemetery, where another crowd had collected. The grave where Mr. Muller's body was buried was an ordinary one on the slope of a hill, under the shade of a yew tree, and was by the side of his first and second wives. Mr. G. F. Bergin spoke from the words, *"By the grace of God, I am what I am"* (I Cor. 15:10).

The crowd gathered around to view for the last time the coffin on which was inscribed, *"George Muller, fell asleep 10th March, 1898, in his 93rd year."*

In every pulpit in Bristol and in thousands across the world on the Sunday before the burial, memorial services were conducted and loving tributes were offered in memory of this man of trust. Friends wanted to erect an expensive monument over his grave but this Mr. Wright would not permit. Later gifts from many orphans flowed in and a simple marker was erected therefore, on which was a tribute of love to this man who through faith had cared for about ten thousand orphans.

His monument was not to be in marble, but in the hearts of loving followers, many of whom had preceded him to Heaven—the thousands of orphans he had fed and clothed—the multitudes who had been taught in Sunday schools due to his prayer diligence — those brought to the Master on mission fields through workers who had been supported by his prayer generosity—and the millions who had read the Scriptures and tracts which his faith provided.

This is a monument more lasting than granite—a monument eternal in the heavens.

Chapter XIV

HIS LENGTHENING SHADOW

When Mr. Muller died his work was not at an end, but slowly with the passing years the shadow of his life lengthened. The setting sun struck his spiritual stature and cast the broad outlines of his noble existence upon the coming decades. Today, Mr. Muller, though dead, still lives through the monumental work he left behind.

That question, *What of the future?* held no terrors for Mr. Muller's successors so long as they remained true to the foundation principles. James Wright declared in his funeral oration, *It is going on!* And today, these many years since its founder's death, it still triumphs through faith. God buried His workers, several of them since that time, but His work carries on.

"I am no prophet," Mr. Wright said in that funeral oration, "but when I remember the prayers which my beloved mother-in-law and father-in-law offered for years for the future of this work . . . that He in His way would raise up some help or helpers to share the responsibility of the work, and when I remember that that has been the theme of our united supplications, I cannot believe that the blessed God, Who has so illustrated His faithfulness in this work for sixty-four years, is going to leave those prayers unanswered.

"But, as I say, what He does will be worthy of Himself. I would only ask the prayers of all believers on behalf of the little group of workers up at the Orphan Houses . . . for prayer is the appointed means to get the blessing."

God did raise up that first worker in the form of Mr. Wright, who entered upon the responsibilities with no fear of the future. For two or more years before Mr. Muller's death there was a great trial of faith. Some of those months were seasons of dire need. It is recorded that on two mornings the mailman did not bring a single donation . . . *the only experience of its kind in fifty years.* Nine days before Mr. Muller's home-going the flood gates of blessings were opened and a sum of £1,427 was received. "How gracious," Mr. Wright said, "it was of the Lord to order that these hundreds of petitions should be answered nine days before his home-call."

While Mr. Muller's death brought no financial legacy, it did leave a more valuable gift in the form of unanswered prayers, which petitions were soon to be heartily answered by the Lord. For within the next few months thousands of pounds came in as donations, which Mr. Wright felt his deceased father-in-law had prayed in before his death.

Mr. Wright was burdened about a fellow-workman, with whom he could share the responsibilities of the Houses, so he gave himself to much prayer. God seemed to indicate that George Frederick Bergin, with whom he had been intimately acquainted for twenty-five years should take this position.

When he presented the matter to Mr. Bergin, he found that this person was on his way to offer his services in such a capacity. The Spirit had put it on his heart that here was to be his sphere of labor.

In 1899 a letter came from a total stranger who wanted to know how the finances of the Institution stood, but Mr. Wright answered that it was against the principles of the work to divulge the financial status to any one. These matters were in the hands of God. By return mail a check for $5,250 arrived from the same person.

The year after Mr. Muller's death the total income was £29,670, and the following year it mounted to £43,985, showing thus that the blessings of God were still upon the work and those who bore its burdens. During the years from 1900-1904 there was always a substantial balance on hand for the work, and at one time this balance ran to more than $57,000.

On January 29, 1905, after a long illness, Mr. Wright died in his seventy-ninth year and was buried near the spot where his father-in-law rested. During his life it was often supposed that he had a private source of income, so great were his gifts. But Mr. Bergin found the secret of his liberality.

"On examining his cash books," Mr. Bergin wrote, "I discovered it was his regular habit to lay aside, of every gift he received . . . not a tenth, not a fifth, not a quarter, but a *half*. This large proportion did not satisfy him, for I found that out of what I may call his own half, he gave liberally, in addition to giving all the Lord's portion."

His total estate, counting personal effects and cash, amounted to $230. And his doctrine, "Owe no man anything," was fulfilled, for all he owed were his doctor, the undertaker and the lawyer's fee for proving his will.

Thus seven years after Mr. Muller's death the active control of the Orphan Houses along with all the other labors of the Institution fell upon the shoulders of one who had not been connected with its founder. The public often wondered how the work would progress, and whether or not God would abundantly supply the needs as he had done heretofore.

It required $3,500 a week to operate the home alone, and during those first weeks often only half that amount came in, but when the 1905 books were balanced, they showed a surplus of $175, with a total income of £25,980.

Mr. Bergin knew but one way to proceed and that was the Muller-way of clinging to the Lord. "Put yourself if you can . . . in our position—over 1,900 orphan children to feed, clothe, and educate . . . and see how truly we had to look to, yea, cling to, our God, as the ivy clings to the oak tree, and is by it supported in the storm."

Many were the miraculous answers to his prayers, as they had been to the prayers of the founder. On September 27, 1905, the Centenary of Mr. Muller's birth was celebrated, and Mr. Bergin asked the Lord to supply 2,000 bananas for the children's cakes. He sent to town to find out the price, and while the messenger was gone 4,000 bananas arrived. "So through God's bounty, our children had two bananas each on the 27th, whereas I had only thought of one each— 'exceeding abundantly above all we ask or think!' "

At the beginning of 1907 Mr. Bergin and his son, a physician, were riding in a Bristol street car when they saw a request for $12,500 for local medical charity. "I pointed it out to my son remarking that this was about what we needed and that the Lord could give us that sum *without any public appeal.*"

So in private and public prayer they asked God to send in these funds, and "It is worthy to note that during the fortnight ending yesterday (9th), while these appeals were facing us, He gave us £2,570 7s. 5½d." (or $350 more than they had asked for).

Large balances were at hand at the close of 1908 and 1909. The first year this balance was practically $24,000 and the second year it was $13,580. Since the Institution was founded in 1834, until May, 1910, £1,820,675 were contributed for the various objects which Mr. Muller wrote into the first statement of the purpose of the work. In the twelve years since Mr. Muller's death £363,522 came in as donations.

Some said that when George Muller passed to his heavenly reward the work would dwindle and finally die. But as long as faith remains the work will continue. Shortly again God was to bury a worker, but faith and the work were to carry on, proving as Mr. Muller often affirmed that *the living God is living still.*

Mr. Frederick Bergin had two sons, both of them doctors. His older son, Dr. G. F. Bergin, was associated with his father for several years, and in 1910 he passed to his reward. The blow was heavy to the father, so on June 1, 1910 he sent to London for his second son, Dr. William M. Bergin, to assist him.

This proved to be a happy partnership, which lasted, however only two years. For in 1912 the elder Bergin died, and left the work to his son. "The blow that fell upon the Institution on October 8, 1912," writes Dr. Bergin, "was the heaviest it had ever sustained. When Mr. Muller was called Home, Mr. Wright had been his helper for over thirty-eight years. When Mr. Wright passed away to be with the Lord, Mr. Bergin had been seven years his colleague. But when my beloved father fell asleep, I had only been two years and four months assisting him. . . . And I saw that if it should please God still to continue the work, it would evidently be a greater proof than ever that 'God is still the living God, and today, as thousands of years ago, he answers the prayers of His believing children.' "

Dr. Bergin had assumed the active leadership only a few months when he took seriously ill, and felt that it would please the Lord to select someone to assist him in carrying the burdens of the Home. He sought God's guidance in the matter, and the decision came that God's choice was Alfred E. Green, a missionary for twenty years in the Straits Settlements, who then was waiting upon the Lord for guidance to return to his former labors.

When Dr. Bergin presented the thought to Mr. Green, he asked for time in which to seek the mind of the Spirit. Duly he came to the decision that this was to be God's work henceforth for him. The association proved to be a happy one, for many years, until Dr. Bergin's death on March 31, 1930. It was greatly crowned with God's benedictions, for through those years every need was supplied.

"As ever, our appeals are made to God alone," writes Mr. Green. "Very grave have been the circumstances of this country and of the world during these past years; but the resources of God are boundless, and he had maintained these Homes to witness . . . to his power and his willingness to answer believing prayer in every time of need."

During the first World War when everything seemed darkest, God always arrived in time with a bounteous supply of the needs. While the banks closed, God sent in sufficient funds to purchase what might be necessary to feed the children.

On August 14, 1914, this entry is found in the Report: "These are the things which faced us this morning on one side, and on the other was our responsibility in caring for the 1677 children today in these Homes, with also the 200 workers employed. . . . But seeing that for three days (when the banks were closed) we shall not be able to draw any money from the bank, how shall we do? This is soon answered by the Lord, for one of the first letters to be opened contained a £100 Bank of England note, with the simple wording, '£100 for the Orphanage, from Bath.' . . . Altogether today we have nearly fifty gifts . . . and the total amounted to £172 13s. 7d. So indeed we thanked God and took courage."

In the Report for 1914-15 Dr. Bergin made this statement, "So graciously has the Lord supplied our needs during the year that we conclude it with a balance of £12,016 7s. 6½d." During the year following the Lord graciously supplied all current needs so that this surplus was not touched, and Dr. Bergin states, "It seems to us as if He has been saying, 'You see, my children, that though I did leave you a large balance, it was just as easy for Me to continue to supply all your needs as to allow you to draw upon your balance.'"

In January, 1917, it became necessary for the Home to buy their annual supply of oatmeal, which amounted to ten tons. They discovered the price was four times the pre-war price, and there was little money on hand for this purchase. After praying about the matter Dr.

Bergin and Mr. Green decided it was God's will for them to contract for the oatmeal.

"Almost the first letter opened at Ashley Down," states Mr. Green, in recalling the incident, "contained a banker's draft for £156 from Australia. . . . Thus the Lord confirmed our faith by showing His ability to send us help in this time of need from the other end of the world."

These wonderful provisions continued from God's hand and even in the smallest details the Home was not overlooked however dark the conditions might have been. Once the government commandeered a $1,750 consignment of oatmeal from America, just at the time when the Home greatly needed the supply. The group of workers went to their knees in prayer, and soon God answered by the ringing of the telephone and a word from a government agent saying that shortly another supply would arrive, which they were to receive free of charge.

When the Armistice was signed, Dr. Bergin records that during those stressful years of war God did not suffer them to want. They finished the war-years with a surplus of more than $17,500 in their treasury. "Well may we rejoice to 'talk of all his wondrous works,' and show how practical a thing it is to trust in the '*Living God*,'" says Dr. Bergin.

On March 18, 1922, God sent the largest single gift ever to be received in the long history of the work in the form of a donation from the United States of $45,000. A simple statement accompanied the money, saying, "Please accept this slight token in the Name of our Lord Jesus Christ. Yours by grace only."

On the 29th of the same month another check for $6,135.67 arrived. About this Dr. Bergin writes,

"Surely we are proving that our God is able to open the windows of heaven for us." During the four days of April 24-27, God sent in a total of more than $50,000, or £12,296.

The happy relation of Mr. Green and Dr. Bergin was broken by the doctor's death on March 31, 1930. His last days had been times of severe suffering, but through the pain his faith triumphed. In this distressful time Mr. Green selected his brother-in-law, Thomas Tilsley, to be his colleague in carrying on the work.

The latest Report of the Institution was issued in 1939, giving the income for the year 1938-39. This showed a total income for the Orphanage fund of £34,322 8s. 9d. There was also a balance on hand of £7 124s. 9½d. Thus God, the Living God, has been able to supply all the needs of the Home. The Report concludes:

"Without anyone having been personally applied to by us for a donation, £2,369,747 12s. 8¾d. has been received for the Orphans, *as a result of prayer to God,* since the commencement of the work, which sum includes the amount received for the Building Fund for the five Houses. Besides this, articles of clothing, furniture, etc., and of food have been given in great variety for the use of the Orphans."

To this must be added another £507,499 which has been donated for other phases of the work. From the sale of Bibles came £35,341, and of tracts and books an additional £68,963, and by payment of children in the day schools the sum of £25,377. For the free distribution of the *Autobiography* of Mr. Muller there has been recieved £539 7s.

"Thus it will be seen that up to the present time,"

the Report continues, "*the Living God* has sent in answer to prayer £3,007,469 12s. 3d."

The present director of the Houses, Mr. Alfred Green, comments on this figure, "Think quietly over that large figure. And consider whether Mr. Muller has not been fully justified in his setting out, in a path of utter dependence upon God alone, to give a visible proof that God would show Himself to be still the Living God."

Humanly speaking it is utterly impossible to think of this amount of money being received without asking anyone for a contribution. The total money thus received during 105 years since Mr. Muller founded the Scriptural Knowledge Institution is the staggering sum of $15,037,348.

Looking into the future Mr. Green and Mr. Tilsley asked the Lord to raise up another assistant to help in carrying the heavy load of the Institution and the Lord made clear his choice in the person of John McCready. A lengthy career in banking combined with the necessary spiritual qualifications of a love for the Bible as well as sincere faith mark him as God's man for this hour of stress.

The selection of workers to carry on the Institution is most important, for as one falls by the wayside a younger one must assume the responsibility for the Houses and other objects of the Institution. Since the chain of prayer must remain unbroken, it would be a calamity to appoint one not evidently called of God and set apart for the work of being a successor to Mr. Muller, the man of trust.

These war days, once again upon England, will prove hard for the Orphanage. But the living God is living still as He was during the fateful period of 1914-18, at which time each Report showed God had not only sent the necessary funds for the work, but had also provided a yearly surplus.

The shadow of Mr. Muller lengthens into the future. The work he founded continues to carry Gospel truth to the ends of the earth. Though present with the Lord his influence increases with the passing days. This man of trust stands as an example of what God will do with one who is fully consecrated to Him.